"Too many Christians marry each other believing being Christian is enough to guarantee a successful marriage, but there's nothing further from the truth. *Marriage without Misery* does a masterful job of challenging all people to realize the necessity of putting in the work to have a successful marriage . . . Many books identify biblical principles associated with marriage, but *Marriage without Misery* takes the next step to help readers *apply* the biblical principles to their marriages to combat the proclivity to sinful actions and attitudes that results in self-centered living. Knowing Jesus and practicing the scriptural principles in this book will put you on the path to experiencing a marriage without misery."

—D. Z. COFIELD
Senior Pastor, Good Hope Missionary Baptist Church

"I am so proud of Darrell and Cynthia Rose for their exceptional book. As long as I have known them, they have been providing effective counsel to others while glorifying God in their own marriage. Their book is immensely practical, thoroughly biblical, and deeply compassionate in how it confronts the challenges of marriage. Be sure to read it with an open Bible and a highlighter as well as a pen because the information in this book has the power to be used by God to transform the most miserable marriages for his glory."

—JOSEPH PARLE
Provost and Senior Professor, College of Biblical Studies

"This interactive book can help you think in a deeper way about God and his principles for a Christ-honoring, fulfilling marriage. It is biblically based and practical, helpful both for those who are considering marriage and those who want to strengthen their marriage."

—RICH THOMSON
Author of *The Heart of Man and the Mental Disorders*

"Darrell and Cynthia Rose have skillfully written a marriage manuscript to help couples navigate through the minefields of disorder . . . Darrell and Cynthia's experience, commitment to couples, and reliance on the Word of God have given them pearls of wisdom for those seeking to strengthen their relationships and those who are contemplating getting married. Their step-by-step approach to navigating through marital pitfalls has laid the foundation for couples who are having difficult times to have a resource to understand how to redirect their marriage. It also gives those who are contemplating marriage a great understanding of what it will take to have a God-ordained marriage. This is certainly a resource tool for Christians who love God's Word and have the responsibility of working with couples. *Marriage without Misery* is a must-read."

— **WILLIE RICHARDSON**
Senior Pastor and Founder, Christian Stronghold
Baptist Church, Philadelphia

Marriage without Misery

Marriage without Misery

How to Move from Chaos to Conformity in Christ

Darrell *and* Cynthia Rose

Foreword by Willie Richardson

RESOURCE *Publications* · Eugene, Oregon

MARRIAGE WITHOUT MISERY
How to Move from Chaos to Conformity in Christ

Resource Publications
An Imprint of Wipf and Stock Publishers
199 W. 8th Ave., Suite 3
Eugene, OR 97401

www.wipfandstock.com

PAPERBACK ISBN: 978-1-6667-0589-8
HARDCOVER ISBN: 978-1-6667-0590-4
EBOOK ISBN: 978-1-6667-0591-1

08/20/21

Contents

Foreword

DARRELL AND CYNTHIA ROSE have skillfully written a marriage manuscript to help couples navigate through the minefields of disorder. They use biblical principles and precepts to lay out the standards for happy, successful marriages. The Roses' teaching of the application of the Word of God in marriage unfolds a blueprint designed to enhance, build, support, and improve the quality of marriage relationships as God intended. What makes this book so different is the use of actual personal cases that have been flatten, so no one is identifiable. The issues, struggles, disappointments, devastations, numbness, hopes, love, anger, joys, hurt, pain, disillusionment, the struggle for self-reliance, and the pure heart to want to do the right thing in God's eye, are all present in this book. This book displays the human condition and experience and paints an accurate picture of the struggles of numerous couples in many different situations with a plan for restoration and redemption.

What is delightful in this manuscript is the subtle understanding that even good marriages can become great marriages. The notion is, in every marriage, there is always something to work on. Good marriages can get stuck and, at some point, accept the mediocracy that sets in. People tend to admire couples who have been married for a long time. The assumption is they really love each other. For many, that is the case, but for others, they are suffering in silence. Certainly, God intends for marriage to belong and be a place to find fulfillment. God ordained marriage, so he knows it is important for marriages to thrive until death departs them. Just because the words until death do you part are no longer used consistently does not mean God no longer intends for this model of unity, love, and respect to thrive until their departure from one another. God absolutely wants marriages to be an example on earth of what a covenant union looks like. *Marriage without Misery* addresses this issue by giving instructions on how to make your good marriage become even better.

The Roses' experience, commitment to couples, and reliance on the Word of God have given them pearls of wisdom for those seeking to strengthen their relationships and to those who are contemplating getting married. This couple's real experience helps them lay a foundation of information for all people trying to gather the information they need that is crucial to fortifying their unions. Darrell and Cynthia's step-by-step approach to navigating through marital pitfalls has laid the foundation for couples who are having difficult times to have a resource to understand how to redirect their marriage.

One of the poignant approaches in this book is examining the heart of the matter, which is addressed by the fall of man. Sin enters the picture anytime we assert our rights over another. Thereby allowing self-interest, self-desire, and self-gratification to reign in the hearts of men and women. Really this makes sense. Each time husbands and wives are out of fellowship with one another, isn't it because one person has valued their own being over another? Divine love, as demonstrated by Jesus Christ, is sacrificial. The Roses challenges the reader to self-examination to see if the origin of the problem has emerged from our sinful nature.

More importantly, this book helps rescue naïve, unsuspecting couples contemplating marriage to understand what marriage really takes to be successful. It provides couples with tangible resources to start the real work long before the marriage takes place. This approach will save many marriages from divorce and may point out to couples they are not ready to get married. Or perhaps, help them to understand they are marrying the wrong person. These are all important principles and precepts. It also gives those who are contemplating marriage a great understanding of what it will take to have a God-ordained marriage.

The Roses speak of this book as a practical approach to living in a marriage. The Roses are not just telling you what to do to promote a good relationship but are also telling you how to have a great relationship following biblical perspective. This accomplishment fulfills one of the objectives set out by these authors "to help couples establish a solid biblical foundation for marriage so that they can have a biblical perspective on the origin and function of marriage." The Roses understand the Bible is still the most important book on the planet when it comes to the marriage relationship, which was instituted and ordained by God.

This book is an excellent tool for Pastors, Counselors, church leadership who tend to be the first to respond (first responders) to people who are having difficulty in their relationships. However, individuals, couples, small groups of all types, and even sharing with your neighbor and friends would benefit from the information in this book. Having a resource like this is a game-changer. This is an easy read, principles, and precepts from the Bible are explained easily. Hearing what other couples have faced shows others they are not the only ones struggling. The different kinds of cases give the counselor a capable tool to use in their sessions. If you serve in a counseling capacity in any area or have the responsibility of working with couples on any level, this book is a natural resource for you. This is undoubtedly a powerful resource tool for Christians who love God, and love God's Word, and want to be effective in working with couples. Marriage without Misery is a must-read if one of your responsibilities is to shepherd couples through the most challenging times in their marriage.

Rev. Dr. Willie Richardson
Senior Pastor and Founder
Christian Stronghold Baptist Church
Philadelphia, PA

Acknowledgements

SOME PEOPLE HAVE ASKED us how long it took to write this book. We typically say nearly two and a half years. This book is a culmination of decades and people who have sacrificed and sown in our lives even if they did not realize it. We want to thank some of those who had an impact on our journey to completing this book. Sometimes one does not realize how much people have sown into their lives until God leads them to do a work that they were not completely prepared to do before the teaching, help, influence, and inspiration of those that contributed to their growth.

First, we are thankful for our marriage. After more than three decades of being married, we are still enamored with one another, grateful to God for each other and for how he has allowed us to be a blessing to others. We realize that it is not always easy to work together and consistently strive to be selfless as a team, void of conflict. Yet, God enabled us to come together as one flesh to produce a book about how to have a marriage without misery using our different ideas, preferences, and gifts to his glory.

We want to thank our sons Aaron and Jonathan for their sacrifice and patience for having two parents ministering, counseling others, and spending a lot of time on computers without complaining. Our prayer is that we have been a godly example and that your lives reflect the love and dedication to the Lord we have modeled.

We want to say thank you to hundreds of married and premarital couples who allowed us to counsel them over the years. You let us into your lives, shared your struggles and pain with transparency. We are grateful you allowed us the opportunity to help you strengthen your marriages and prepare you for the lifelong commitment to the Divine covenant of Holy matrimony. We are also thankful for those of you who allowed us to walk with you through the process of healing and restoration.

Acknowledgements

We want to give a special thanks to our Pastor, Dr. D. Z. Cofield, Sr. Pastor of Good Hope MBC, for allowing us to exercise our spiritual gifts and entrust the ministries of Christian Education, Marriage Enrichment, and Biblical Counseling under our care. We are thankful for the encouragement, support, and pastoral leadership you have given us over the last 25 years. Dr. Cofield, you have been a significant influence on our Christian growth and leadership development.

We want to extend heartfelt gratitude to the leaders of the Christian Stronghold Church and Christian Research & Development in Philadelphia, Pa. We want to thank Rev. Dr. Willie Richardson, Senior Pastor and Founder, and Dr. Annette V. Hampton, Executive Director of Alpha Community Development Corporation. The Biblical Counseling training curriculum that you all provided was the spark that ignited our journey. Since then, we have taken over 400 counseling cases. As a result, our experience with numerous married and premarital counseling cases has led and prepared us to write this book.

We want to thank College of Biblical Studies Houston Professors Dr. Rich Thompson, author of "The Heart of Man and the Mental Disorders," and founder of the Biblical Framework Counselors Association, for your instruction, mentoring, humble inspiration, and Dr. Joe Parle for his tireless efforts of teaching, mentoring, encouraging students and edifying Christians for the work of the Kingdom.

Many thanks to The Master's University and Seminary in Santa Clarita, California Professors Dr. John Street and Dr. Bob Sommerville, and Biblical Counseling Professors. Your teaching, mentoring, and encouragement have well prepared us for counseling every situation that befalls man, through the all-sufficient, inerrant word of God.

We must say thank you to Copyeditor, Dr. Matthew Bizzell Ph.D., Texas A&M | MA American and British Literature. University of Houston | Ph.D. American and English Literature, who completed the copyediting for our book project. We sincerely appreciate you, Dr. Bizzell, for your expertise in English literature and grammatical proficiency.

We want to thank Wipf and Stock Publishers team; advisor Manager Matthew Wimer, Editorial Production Manager, always patient Rachel Saunders, Typesetter, and the skillful, professional publishing staff.

Introduction

MANY COUPLES TODAY ARE married and miserable. Too many husbands and wives are living together as roommates. The love and passion they once felt for one another has been depleted. Many are disappointed, some are angry, others are bitter, and a few may come to believe there is no hope for their marriage. Unmet expectations, money problems, distrust, and extended family issues have all taken a toll on the marriage and couples are lost on how to resolve them. For some of them, if they do not get help and experience a breakthrough in their marital relationship, divorce will be inevitable.

In almost twenty years of counseling, we have seen many couples who have given up on their marriage even before they come to counseling. The relationship has deteriorated so that counseling is just the final thing to check the box on before divorce papers are filed. Sadly, divorce is more common than ever. In the current culture, many marriages are either dying, dead, or ending in divorce. Divorce tears couples apart emotionally, mentally, and spiritually—it rips at the very heart of a person. For some people, the initial stages of divorce are so painful that their brokenness can be compared to the death of a loved one.

For some, divorce plays out like the attack of an archenemy. Hatred, slander, plotting, and exposing the other's sin are just the start of what occurs in an all out war of revenge and ruin. There is a report of a forty-three-year-old homeowner who went through a contentious divorce. The judge decided to split the couple's possessions right down the middle and ruled that the husband and wife divide their assets equally. So, in a fit of rage, the husband decided to cut their summer house in half with a chainsaw. After finishing the job, he loaded his half onto a forklift and drove it to his brother's house, where he was staying. According to police, the man was merely "taking his due."[1]

Research indicates that one divorce occurs every thirteen seconds in the United States, a statistic that ranks the nation sixth on a global divorce rate scale.[2] An estimated 80 percent of couples, including Christian couples, head in the direction of divorce within their first four to five years of marriage. These sobering statistics might discourage married or engaged couples who are striving to beat the odds, but it is entirely possible to sustain a committed, fulfilled, and intimate union that doesn't succumb to the agonizing reality of divorce.[3] Research implies that this startling, however common, trajectory is often due to decreased passion and excitement in the relationship.[4] This research's conclusion is based on human wisdom.

Although this research may be partially correct regarding the conclusion that many marriages end in divorce, it has failed to identify the root cause of divorce. From a biblical perspective, marriages end in divorce because of sin. Couples sin against God and one another. They are not willing to confess, repent by changing their thinking and behavior, or forgive. People go into marriage to please themselves and not their spouse. They do not understand the purpose of marriage and their roles as a husband and wife. They experience poor communication and fail to deal with unresolved conflict. Some will use the lack of passion and excitement in their marriage to justify having an affair. We all desire passion and excitement in our marriage, but the lack of it is not the cause of divorce. These are merely occasions for discontentment. Some people may use these superficial occasions in an attempt to justify separation.

Couples in trouble may feel that their marriage is beyond hope—but just the opposite is true. Couples need to know that they are not alone and that what they are going through are common issues that other couples experience. The truth is that overcoming what seem to be insurmountable problems may be a difficult task, but it is not impossible. There is hope. There is an absolute path to restoration through God's word when his principles are embraced and applied to your marriage. There is a way to have a marriage without the misery that 80 percent of couples experience and

1. Reuters Life!, "German man chainsaws house"
2. hrf, "55 Surprising Divorce Statistics for Second Marriages"
3. Wevorce Team, "6 Surprising Statistics About Divorce in 2017"
4. The Gottman Institute, "10 Ways to Rekindle the Passion in Your Marriage"

a way to enjoy the journey with a love that encourages, affirms, assures, matures, and glorifies God.

This book, *Marriage without Misery: How to Move from Chaos to Conformity to Christ,* is essential for marriage in the three ways: It is personal, profitable, and practical. It was written to equip those who are considering marriage prepare for marriage. It also provides help, hope, and encouragement to those who are struggling to find healing and restoration. This book is also designed to help good marriages become great marriages.

Marriage without Misery is beneficial first, because it is personal. We use actual counseling situations (though with names changed) from years of counseling cases to present common problems that most couples can relate to and that are relevant to marital relationships. Problems in relationships stem from the heart. In other words, when our natural desires to please ourselves overtake our desires to please God, man is inclined to sin. We instinctively pursue avenues for self-gratification. On the other hand, our love for God and desire to please him is evidenced by our love for others. Our purpose is to help every reader examine themselves, specifically their hearts, through the lens of Scripture.[5]

For troubled marriages, we discovered that concrete change can only occur when a person can identify who they are and be honest with themselves regarding their unloving attitudes, failures, shortcomings, hurts, habits, and hang-ups. Unless a person can see themselves as they are in their current condition from God's perspective, confess, and repent of their sins, there can be no hope for change.

Second, this work is profitable. It contains expositions of fundamental theological principles that are essential for marriage. Second Timothy 3:16–17 says,

> All Scripture is breathed out by God and profitable for teaching,
> for reproof, for correction, and for training in righteousness, that
> the man of God may be complete, equipped for every good work.

Marriage without Misery demonstrates that the word of God is profitable and gives life. God's word invigorates and revitalizes. God's word is beneficial for teaching believers about life and living, particularly marriage. It provides instructions. It warns us against what we should not do. It gives correction when we are wrong. And it is a training manual for living a righteous

---

5. Lamentations 3:40; 2 Corinthians 13:5 (NASB)

life. The result is a husband and wife who are spiritually mature and have the tools they need for the kingdom work that God calls every believer to do.

Lastly, this book is practical. It is a biblical counseling resource of practical theology. In other words, it not only teaches what the word of God says about marital issues, but offers specific ways couples can apply biblical principles to their marriage—it is a vehicle through which couples can learn how to live out these biblical principles in their marriage and family.

Most married couples come to counseling because they are experiencing chaos within their marriage. The most common reasons why couples struggle is because they lack understanding of the purpose of marriage, and have a misunderstanding of their respective roles. They are unwilling to accept differences, experiencing unmet and unrealistic expectations, have unresolved conflict, or experiencing poor communication. Some have chaos with their relationships with in-laws. Other married couples experience disorder in raising children in blended families. Financial struggles can cause havoc in the marriage, and sometimes couples get so absorbed with children's activities or work that they become disconnected and lack intimacy with their spouse.

Here is the good news! This book not only explains what God says about these issues, but it also provides comprehensive ways to apply biblical knowledge to your marriage. Each chapter contains counseling situations (with fictitious names) to illustrate the problem areas, along with Scripture references relevant to each subject. As you and your spouse prepare to take this journey through the content of this book, please remain prayerful for your spouse or fiancée, but also pray for yourself that God will reveal the issues of your own heart that are preventing you from being the husband or wife that God calls you to be. Change begins with self-awareness and understanding your need for grace and mercy, not from your perspective, but from God's perspective.

In summary, it all starts with a reverence for God and a desire to conform to the image of Christ. Conforming to the image of Christ means you must commit to loving your spouse, even if it means that you suffer in your efforts. Husbands must love their wives, even when love is not reciprocated. Wives must submit to their husbands, even if their husbands are unworthy. As you and your spouse grow in the likeness of Christ, you will receive and enjoy God's great rewards that He promises to those who choose to love one another as God loves:

> Give, and it will be given to you. They will pour into your lap a good measure—pressed down, shaken together, *and* running over. For by your standard of measure it will be measured to you in return[6]

The goal for every husband and wife is to reflect the image of God. To love as Christ, to give as Christ gave, and to do good to others—specifically your spouse—even when it is not reciprocated. Fulfilling your role as a husband or wife may require that you suffer. But your suffering is not in vain. It is part of conforming to the image of Christ. The remedy for chaos is conformity, but not merely because it is pleasing to your spouse but because it brings honor to God when you suffer for doing what God has called you to do:

> For what credit is there if, when you sin and are harshly treated, you endure it with patience? But if when you do what is right and suffer *for it*, you patiently endure it, this *finds* favor with God. For you have been called for this purpose, since Christ also suffered for you, leaving you an example for you to follow in His steps, *who committed no sin, nor was any deceit found in his mouth*; and while being reviled, He did not revile in return; while suffering, He uttered no threats, but kept entrusting *Himself* to Him who judges righteously[7]

We challenge you to commit yourself to apply the principles of this book to your marriage. Reading the material alone is never enough without application. If you apply these principles, you can have a marriage without misery and move from chaos to conformity in Jesus Christ. Our hearts and our prayers go out to you and your spouse in the most fervent way—let's take this fantastic journey together. We sincerely appreciate your investment in this material and for allowing us the opportunity to share our gifts and sow into your life and marriage.

We pray for God's Blessings and grace upon you and your spouse. Amen!

---

6. Luke 6:38 (NASB)

7. 1 Peter 2:20–24 (NASB)

1

The Purpose of Marriage

TALK TO ANYONE, AND they will tell you that life has its challenges. You learn to expect the unexpected. Oftentimes you are plagued with problems and difficulties of life on every side. But what is even worse than hard times is facing life alone. A book may be a good companion for a season, watching television or social media may keep you from feeling lonely for a while, and even a walk in the park may be refreshing. But the truth is, all of us have an inner longing for companionship, for someone to take part in what we are thinking, seeing, hearing, and experiencing. We need someone to share our life with.

Objective:

The purpose of this chapter is to help couples establish a solid biblical foundation for marriage so that they can have a biblical perspective on the origin and function of marriage. Having a clear understanding of the purpose of marriage can equip married couples to live according to their God-intended purpose, according to God's design and not man's.

Who and What Defines Marriage?

From the World's Perspective:

From a natural man's perspective, marriage is a human institution; as such, man believes he has the right and the authority to set the guidelines as to what he believes constitutes a marriage and its function as he pleases. The world defines marriage as two individuals living together in agreement of self-defined roles, regardless of sexual gender.

Some support the idea that a man and woman can live together, have children, own a home, and enjoy all the benefits of marriage without living under the title of a married couple. They desire a license-free relationship of living together with the freedom to nullify their living arrangement if they choose to do so.

Some believe that marriage is temporary, so they get married already prepared for divorce on the basis of a "prenuptial agreement." But the truth is, marriage cannot be both divinely instituted and humanly instituted. If marriage was a human institution, then man has the right and the authority to set the guidelines as to what constitutes a marriage and how it should function. Why, because the natural (unregenerate) man believes he is the supreme authority.

From God's Perspective:

> So, the lord God caused a deep sleep to fall upon the man, and he slept; then He took one of his ribs and closed up the flesh at that place. The lord God fashioned into a woman the rib which He had taken from the man, and brought her to the man. The man said, "This is now bone of my bones, And flesh of my flesh; She shall be called Woman, Because she was taken out of Man." For this reason a man shall leave his father and his mother, and be joined to his wife; and they shall become one flesh. And the man and his wife were both naked and were not ashamed.[1]

According to Genesis 2:21–25, who instituted marriage, and why is the answer to this question significant? _____

_____

_____

1. Genesis 2:21–25 (NASB)

The Creator of Marriage has the Sole Authority to Define Marriage:

The children of Israel asked the prophet Malachi why God was no longer accepting their offerings of worship; he answered them saying: "Yet you say, 'For what reason?' Because the lord has been a witness between you and the wife of your youth, against whom you have dealt treacherously, though she is your companion and your wife by covenant."[2]

Marriage is a Covenant of Companionship:

> To deliver you from the strange woman, From the adulteress who flatters with her words; That leaves the companion of her youth And forgets the covenant of her God[3]

What is meant by the word "covenant" and why is this significant in marriage? _____
_____
_____

What is a Covenant?

The Bible uses the word "covenant" to mean the most solemn and most binding agreement made between man to man and man to God. An example of a covenant can be seen in the life of Abraham in Genesis 15:8–21. Animals were cut in half and laid opposite of one another.[4] There appeared a burning torch, signifying the presence of God that passed between the halves. If a person passed between the two pieces, one declared that he would keep his promises until death. As such, marriage was designed by God as a covenant unto death.

A covenant, in ancient times, involved several elements:

- There was a written agreement.
- There was something tangible as a reminder of the promise made.

2. Malachi 2:14 (NASB)
3. Proverbs 2:16–17 (NASB)
4. Genesis 15:10 (NASB)

- It was done in the presence of witnesses.

- Audible words to the terms of the covenant were exchanged.

- It was done in the presence of the Lord.

1. Are these elements of a covenant descriptive of something familiar; how so? _____

_____

_____

2. What are some of the reasons why most people do not view divorce as a broken covenant? _____

_____

_____

What is the Primary Purpose of Marriage?

From the World's Perspective:

Human wisdom or Secular reasoning will suggest that the purpose of marriage is to:

- Fulfill one's sexual desire.

- Instill self-gratification.

- Acquire significance.

- Satisfy personal needs.

- Add meaning and give identity to one's life.

- Be happy.

- Be secure and accepted.

- Remove despair and isolation.

- Be a cure for loneliness.

- Be a financial investment.

From God's Perspective:

> Then God said, "Let Us make man in Our image, according to Our likeness; and let them rule over the fish of the sea and over the birds of the sky and over the cattle and over all the earth, and over every creeping thing that creeps on the earth." God created man in His own image, in the image of God He created him; male and female He created them.[5]

Read and compare Genesis 1:26 with Genesis 1:27. How are they different from one another?

1. Clue: consider the pronouns: _____
   _____
   _____

2. Who is "Us" in Genesis 1:26? _____
   _____
   _____

Read the following Scripture:

> The man said, "This is now bone of my bones, And flesh of my flesh; She shall be called Woman, Because she was taken out of Man." For this reason a man shall leave his father and his mother, and be joined to his wife; and they shall become one flesh.[6]

1. How does Genesis 2:23–24 relate to Genesis 1:26–27? _____
   _____
   _____

2. The purpose of a mirror is to reflect your image. God created marriage to reflect his image in terms of his person and his character. But what does God's image look like in terms of his person? _____
   _____
   _____

---

5. Genesis 1:26–27 (NASB)
6. Genesis 2:23–24 (NASB)

What is the Image of God's Person?

In Genesis 1:26, the pronouns "Us" and "Our" image are referring to the Father, Son, and Holy Spirit. But in Genesis 1:27, the pronouns "He" and "His" are singular and also include all three divine elements of the Trinity. The Father, Son, and Holy Spirit each possess attributes (Non-communicable), such as omniscience, omnipresence, omnipotence, supreme authority, and sovereignty that only belong to God. God created marriage to reflect his person, which is an image of the co-existence of plurality, oneness, and unity.

What does God's Image Look like in Terms of his Character?

God's character consists of his communicable attributes, including love, joy, graciousness, merciful, forgiving, kindness, intellect, gentleness, and longsuffering. God's communicable attributes are the parts of his nature that he shares with man. Read Colossians 3:12–14 and answer the following questions:

> So, as those who have been chosen of God, holy and beloved, put on a heart of compassion, kindness, humility, gentleness and patience; bearing with one another, and forgiving each other, whoever has a complaint against anyone; just as the Lord forgave you, so also should you. Beyond all these things put on love, which is the perfect bond of unity.[7]

1. How would you describe God's character, according to Colossians 3:12–14? _____
   _____
   _____

2. Consider the answer to this question in light of Jesus. What kind of person is he? How did Jesus respond to God? How did he relate to people? _____
   _____
   _____

3. What kind of a marriage would result if both husband and wife reflected the character of Jesus? _____
   _____
   _____

7. Colossians 3:12–14 (NASB)

Point:

The primary purpose of marriage is to reflect the image of God. It is an image of the person of God, as seen in the character of Jesus Christ!

What is the Secondary Purpose of Marriage?

> Then the lord God said, "It is not good for the man to be alone; I will make him a helper suitable for him."[8]

God said it is not good for man to be alone. He then brought all of the animals to Adam to name but for Adam, a helper suitable to him was not found. Then God caused a deep sleep to fall upon Adam. He took one of Adam's ribs and made woman. Why the delay? God wanted Adam to realize that he needed something. And what Adam needed Adam could not provide for himself. Adam had to learn his dependence upon God to provide what he needed most. It was only then that God put Adam to sleep and provided what he needed.

1. What does the statement "It is not good for man" mean? _____

_____

_____

2. What does it imply about woman? _____

_____

_____

3. What is the alternative to getting married?[9] _____

_____

_____

4. Can a person be married and still be lonely; why or why not? _____

_____

_____

Point:

The secondary purpose of marriage is so that man will not be alone.

8. Genesis 2:18 (NASB)

9. 1 Corinthians 7:7–9 (NASB)

What is the Function of Marriage?

> God blessed them; and God said to them, "Be fruitful and multiply, and fill the earth, and subdue it; and rule over the fish of the sea and over the birds of the sky and over every living thing that moves on the earth."[10]

Most successful business owners have established job descriptions for each position within their companies. A job description is a written account of employee responsibilities, duties, and expectations set forth by the one in charge.

God's job description for the husband and wife is to:

- Be fruitful and multiply.
- Exercise dominion.
- Leave and cleave.
- Become one flesh.
- Fulfill God's kingdom's agenda on Earth.

1. Why does God want man and woman to "be fruitful and multiply?"
   _____
   _____

2. What does it mean to rule over the earth? _____
   _____
   _____

Point:

To be fruitful and multiply is to produce more of the same. In doing so, God's image is magnified. And so is his glory. He wants to look at the Earth and see it filled with himself. God's image is one of supreme authority, so the husband and wife are to reflect God's image by exercising authority.

> Therefore, shall a man leave his father and his mother, and shall cleave unto his wife: and they shall be one flesh.[11]

10. Genesis 1:28 (NASB)
11. Genesis 2:24 (KJV)

One of the most intimate of all human relationships are between parents and their children. There is an emotional, mental, psychological, and spiritual connection that exists between parents and their children. Usually, levels of attachment in relationships occur in this order: first parents, then siblings, family members, friends, and last, acquaintances. But God's job description for marriage is to leave and cleave: leave physically, emotionally, financially, in loyalty and allegiance to one's spouse—the husband and wife are to become one flesh.

1. What does it mean to leave one's "father and mother?" _____
   _____
   _____

2. What does the term "cleave" mean? _____
   _____
   _____

3. We know that "to become one flesh" is a figurative statement. So then, what does it mean practically? _____
   _____
   _____

Point:

Your relationship with your spouse takes precedence over any other human relationship. Your spouse comes first! Oneness and unity are a reflection of God's image.

Summary:

The definition of marriage: marriage was instituted by God and is a covenant of companionship.

The primary purpose of marriage: to reflect the image of God in terms of his person and his character.

The secondary purpose of marriage: to defeat man's loneliness.

The function of marriage: be fruitful and multiply, to exercise dominion, leave and cleave, and become one flesh.

Application:

According to Colossians 3:12–14, as one chosen by God, you are called to put on a heart of love, which is the perfect bond of unity. On a scale of 1 to 5, with five being the best, how well do you reflect the image of God in the following areas? Please rate yourself as well as your mate. Schedule time to discuss and compare answers with your spouse.

Yourself:

_____Compassion: showing sensitivity to those who are suffering and in need.

_____Kindness: nice, thoughtfulness.

_____Humility: thinking lowly of oneself.

_____Gentleness: not behaving harshly, arrogantly.

_____Patience: longsuffering, self-restraining.

_____Bearing with one another: tolerating and putting up with others, enduring discomfort.

_____Forgiving one another: Not holding a grudge or grievance.

Your Mate:

_____Compassion: showing sensitivity to those who are suffering and in need.

_____Kindness: nice, thoughtfulness.

_____Humility: thinking lowly of oneself.

_____Gentleness: not behaving harshly, arrogantly.

_____Patience: longsuffering, self-restraining.

_____Bearing with one another: putting up with others, enduring discomfort.

_____Forgiving one another: Not holding a grudge or grievance.

Love Score:

29–35: Awesome, don't stop what you're doing!

22–28: Good job; get to work on the little things!

15–21: Talk it out, focus on what's missing!

0–14: It's never too late to restore the relationship to the image of God

If you fall short in reflecting the image of God, ask your mate, what can you do to change? Then commit to reflect the love of God, which is the perfect bond of unity.

2

Keeping Your House in Order

The Role of the Husband

Counseling Issue:

JOHN AND SARAH, A married Christian couple, come for biblical counseling. John describes himself as a very hard-working man. He claims he loves his wife because he believes that to love one's wife is to protect her. John thinks that a real man's role is to work hard and provide for his wife and children. As a husband, he feels he has earned his right to be the head and authority in his home.

However, according to Sarah, she does not describe John as a loving man, but as a dictating, demanding, and brutal husband. She is distraught and hurt because of his demands. She feels he is oppressive to her and the children. She says John is insensitive to her feelings and needs. Sarah believes he does not know her or what she needs. She feels unappreciated. Sarah says John ignores her opinions and rejects her input when he makes decisions. She feels devalued and unloved. He often reminds her that he is the man of the house and deserving of her respect.

The Result:

John's demand for respect and his desire to be recognized as the sole authority in his marriage are causing significant problems. John and Sarah are living in the same house, but there is a spiritual and physical disconnect.

There is no peace in the relationship. They are more like rival roommates rather than husband and wife.

The Problem:

John is not fulfilling his biblical role as a husband.

Objective:

To give couples a biblical perspective of how God intended husbands to function within the covenant companionship of marriage. To teach the practice of becoming one flesh and establishing unity so that the marriage will be one that honors God and give peace and harmony to a relationship.

What is Your Role as a Husband?

Ask most men this question, and you will receive a variety of different answers. A few may say their role is to rule their households. Others may believe their purpose is to be the primary decision-maker. Some say they are to share leadership with their wives. The most common answer to this question is that husbands believe their role to be a protector and provider. That sounds good, but being a protector and provider does not capture the primary role of the husband. Let's examine why.

The Traditional View of a Husband's Role:

In America, leading into the 1900s, men were the dominant figures in the home as well as the workplace. Ninety-five percent of wives remained at home, and their job was to care for the children and run the household while the husband worked outside of the house. It was the norm for husbands not to show emotions, or mental or physical weakness. They were expected to show strength, confidence, and be self-reliant. Contemporary culture would view a husband as a disgrace if he did not provide for his family, even in illness.

Today, most households consist of husbands and wives who both work outside of the home. Presently, many husbands and wives are equally-educated and have professional careers. Over the last sixty years, a lot has changed in our society regarding the equality of men and women. Women have made tremendous progress and are enormous contributors to the betterment of our country, whether it be politically, socially, or economically. Yet, despite the achievements of women, some men still hold to the traditional view of the husband's role in marriage.

A husband's demand to be recognized as the authority can cause major marital problems. Many couples end up in counseling, struggling to figure out why there is a disconnect in their marital relationship.

The Biblical View of a Husband's Role:

A husband's role is to love his wife. Scripture says,

> Husbands, love your wives, just as Christ also loved the church and gave Himself up for her, so that He might sanctify her, having cleansed her by the washing of water with the word, that He might present to Himself the church in all her glory, having no spot or wrinkle or any such thing; but that she would be holy and blameless. So husbands ought also to love their own wives as their own bodies. He who loves his own wife as for no one ever hated his own flesh, but nourishes and cherishes it, just as Christ also *does* the church[1]

Scripture also says,

> *For this reason a man shall leave his father and mother and shall be joined to his wife, and the two shall become on* flesh. This mystery is great; but I am speaking with reference to Christ and the church. Nevertheless, each individual among you also is to love his own wife even as himself, and the wife must *see to it* that she respects her husband.[2]

1. According Ephesians 5:25, what is the first thing the husband is commanded to do? _____

_____

_____

---

1. Ephesians 5:25–29 (NASB)
2. Ephesians 5:31–33 (NASB)

2. In verse 25, what did Christ do to demonstrate his love for the church?

_____

_____

3. According to verses 26–27, what was Jesus's reason for loving the church? _____

_____

_____

4. What does it mean to nourish and cherish one's own body, and how does that relate to loving your wife? _____

_____

_____

> Therefore be imitators of God, as beloved children; and walk in love, just as Christ also loved you and gave Himself up for us, an offering and a sacrifice to God as a fragrant aroma.[3]

5. In light of Ephesians 5:1–2, you are commanded to walk in love. As you examine this verse, what does giving, offering, and sacrifice have to do with love? _____

_____

_____

Point 1:

A husband's primary role is to love his wife as Christ loved the church, demonstrated by sacrifice and giving: true love is sacrifice.

A Husband's Role is to Know His Wife:

> You husbands in the same way, live with *your wives* in an understanding way, as with someone weaker, since she is a woman; and show her honor as a fellow heir of the grace of life, so that your prayers will not be hindered.[4]

3. Ephesians 5:1–2 (NASB)
4. 1 Peter 3:7 (NASB)

What does the phrase, "in the same way" mean in this text? To answer this question, go back and read verses before verse 7. _____

_____

_____

First Peter 2:20 says,

> For what credit is there if, when you sin and are harshly treated, you endure it with patience? But if when you do what is right and suffer *for it* you patiently endure it, this *finds* favor with God.

Then Peter closes the rest of chapter 2, describing how Christ suffered for righteousness sake, giving us an example to follow. To paraphrase, 1 Peter 3:7 says, you husbands, in the same way that Christ suffered for righteousness, you too live with your wives doing what is right, even if you have to suffer.

1. What does it mean "to live with" your wife? _____

   _____

   _____

2. How can you live with your wife in an understanding way? What is it that you need to understand?

   About God? _____

   _____

   _____

   About your wife? _____

   _____

   _____

Example:

The key to passing final exams is to study. If you are going to understand your wife, then you must study her. You need to know your wife physically, emotionally, spiritually, and mentally. You should know her strengths, weaknesses, fears, likes, and dislikes. Not only must you live with her in an understanding way, but you must also be mindful that she is the weaker vessel.

Let's examine 1 Peter 3:7, a little further:

You husbands in the same way, live with your wives in an understanding way, as with someone weaker, since she is a woman; and show her honor as a fellow heir of the grace of life, so that your prayers will not be hindered.

1. What does the phrase, "as someone weaker," mean? _____
_____
_____

2. The word "honor" means to esteem. How can you honor your wife and why? _____
_____
_____

3. What are the consequences for failing to understand and honor your wife? _____
_____
_____

Point 2:

A husband's role is to live with and know his wife, honoring her and handling her with care, as someone who is fragile and easily broken.

A Husband's Role is to Lead His Wife:

He must be one who manages his own household well, keeping his children under control with all dignity[5]

In context, 1 Timothy 3:4 speaks of the requirements of the office of an overseer in the church. However, the principles stated are also applicable to a godly husband:

- A godly leader is not a dictator, nor demanding or dominating.
- A godly leader is a compassionate, caring manager of the home and is always concerned about what is in the best interest of the family.
- A godly leader is the head of his family.

5. 1 Timothy 3:4 (NASB)

> But I want you to understand that Christ is the head of every man, and the man is the head of a woman, and God is the head of Christ.[6]

According to 1 Corinthians 11:3, God has established a standard of hierarchy in the marital relationship. The word of God has, by no means, ever stated that the husband is more worthy than the wife. The husband's call to be the leader does not mean that the wife is less significant than the husband. The headship of the husband and the submission of the wife are merely standards of divine function and not the measure of one's worth.

In Genesis, God created Adam first, then Eve.[7] God placed Adam in the Garden of Eden and gave Adam instructions on what he could and could not eat. God told Adam, and Adam told Eve. But Eve disobeyed first, then Adam. They heard the sound of the Lord approaching, and they hid themselves. The Lord called out to Adam, "Where are you?"

In light of Genesis 3:8-9, what do you believe was God's reason for calling Adam when they were both guilty of disobedience? _____

_____

_____

God holds you more accountable for the marriage than your wife because you are the leader.

> *He must be* one who manages his own household well, keeping his children under control with all dignity[8]

If you have a poor dining experience at a restaurant, typically you do not ask to speak to the cook who prepared the meal nor the waiter who served the meal. No. You usually ask for the manager. Why? Because he is responsible for the product, even though he may not have prepared or serviced the meal himself. He is the one in charge. Although your wife is not your employee, you are still called to manage your home.

---

6. 1 Corinthians 11:3 (NASB)

7. Genesis 2:7 (NASB)

8. 1 Timothy 3:4 (NASB)

What is Godly Leadership?

1. What are the responsibilities of a manager? _____
   _____
   _____

2. As you lead, how can you demonstrate the love of God for your wife?
   _____
   _____

Point 3:

A husband's role is to be a godly leader who values his wife's thoughts, opinions, concerns, and needs. He protects and provides for his family.

A Summary of the Role of the Husband:

Point 1:

A husband's primary role is to love his wife as Christ loved the church, demonstrated by sacrifice and giving.

Point 2:

A husband's role is to live with and know his wife, honoring her and handling her with care, as someone who is easily broken.

Point 3:

A husband's role is to be a godly leader who values his wife's thoughts, opinions, concerns, and needs. He protects and provides.

Application Questions:

If your role as a husband is to love your wife as Christ loved the church, then you need to know what that looks like in practice. What kind of person is Jesus? How did he respond to people in need? How did Christ relate to others?

How did he react to his enemies, those who opposed him, cursed him, and falsely accused him? On several occasions, Jesus provided the answer as to why he was doing the things that he did. What reason did Jesus give?

Read the following verses and describe how Jesus demonstrated love in each situation:

1. Matthew 15:30–37: _____

    _____

    _____

2. John 13:5–12: _____

    _____

    _____

3. Matthew 9:9–11: _____

    _____

    _____

4. Luke 6:27–36: _____

    _____

    _____

Why did Jesus love others in this way?

Jesus said on three occasions: I am come to do "the will of Him Who sent Me!"[9] Love involves both attitude and actions.[10] The Apostle Paul also wrote this command to husbands: "Husbands, love your wives and do not be embittered against them."[11]

1. What does Paul mean by, "do not be embittered" against your wife? __

    _____

    _____

2. What are some other bad (unloving) attitudes that can get in the way of you loving your wife? _____

    _____

    _____

Love your wife as Christ loved the church. In doing so, you will find favor with God and your rewards will be great.[12]

9. John 6:38 (NASB)
10. 1 Corinthians 13:4–7 (NASB)
11. Colossians 3:19 (NASB)
12. 1 Peter 2:18–12 (NASB)

Food for Thought:

A husband is the man who loves me beyond measure.

Here is an ambitious acronym for the word "husband":

He lifts me up when I am down.

Understands me like no other.

Supports my every dream.

Believes in me no matter what.

Accepts me, flaws and all.

Nurtures my heart and soul.

Darn near perfect![13]

Do you want a wife who lifts you up when you are down? A wife who seeks to understand you even when she does not agree? A wife who supports your every dream and puts you before herself? A wife who believes in you no matter what? A wife who accepts you as you are, along with your flaws? A wife who is near perfect? How much better would your relationship be if your wife was perfect in all of these areas? But the point is, you should love your wife to the same degree that you want her to love you.

Jesus Christ loves you in the same way. He supports your every dream as long as your desires and dreams line up with the Will of the Father. Will you commit to loving your wife in the same way that Christ loves you? Will you love your wife the same way you want to be loved? If you do, your rewards will be great![14]

13. Happywivesclub.com
14. Luke 6:35 (NASB)

3

Keeping Your House in Order

The Role of the Wife

The Circumstances:

"BUT HE HAD AN affair," the distraught young woman cried as she fought to compose herself. She had sought counseling because she was struggling with a myriad of emotions, including a lack of trust, disappointment, anger, and feeling hurt because her husband Ed had committed adultery. This affair had happened two years ago, and although Bella decided to stay in the marriage, she had concluded that her staying was an act of mercy. Along with the act of mercy, she exercised a level of caution and put her husband on continuous notice that she had a biblical right to divorce him. Since she decided to stay, she would wield power over him. After all, according to this wife, "*he's* the one who broke the marriage covenant."

The Result:

After the affair, Bella and Ed, both Christians, attended biblical counseling. Two years later, Ed stated that Belinda was disrespecting him and failing to submit to his authority as head of the home, and he was fed up. Bella assumed her husband's past sin gave her license to be controlling, demanding, and to challenge his authority and headship in the home.

The Problem:

Bella had a distorted view and a misinterpretation of Scripture concerning submission. There is no cancellation clause for submission. She failed to understand that if she chose to stay in the marriage, she must resolve to respect her husband in his position, and submit to him in everything or she would be in sin. Bella was not fulfilling her role as a wife.

Objective:

The purpose of this section is to correct misconceptions about submission, explain the truths about the biblical role of a wife, and to define the wife's role and demonstrate what it looks like in practice. This chapter will encourage the wife to embrace her role and honor God, resulting in the blessings of obedience, and produce unity, peace, and harmony in her marriage relationship.

What is Your Role as a Wife?

Like husbands, wives may define their role in several different ways. Some may say their role as a wife includes being an equal partner in helping provide for the home and make decisions. Others may say their role includes having children and taking care of household duties. Modern wives may say their role is what they define it to be—whatever fits their lifestyle. The way you define your role will largely depend on what you understand and believe about the Bible. Often, even Christian wives don't know or struggle with embracing their biblical role. We'll discuss why that's so.

Marriage today has been redefined into many meanings, roles, and functions. One thing for sure is that there's no standard, from the world's perspective, of what defines a good marriage. What works for the individual couple is how a good marriage is defined—that is not how God designed marriage to be. Since God instituted marriage in his creation design,[1] he should be the standard of what defines marriage and be the resource Christian couples turn to in order to learn how to live, function, and find real joy in a marriage relationship. Wives can know their purpose, role, and function in a Christ-led marriage through God's infallible, sufficient word.

1. Genesis 2 (NASB)

1. What do you believe your role is as a wife? _____

   _____

   _____

2. Who or what influenced you to think this way? _____

   _____

   _____

The Traditional View of a Wife's Role:

A wife's traditional role was to stay at home, birth and nurture children, manage domestic duties, and attend to the husband's needs. In the 1800s, before the Civil War, the Women's Suffrage Movement started as a political campaign for women's right to vote and for political equality. Over the next decade, other reform movements started with women playing a prominent role. By the 1960s, The Women's Liberation Movement was born. Feminism, as it has come to be known, is defined as the advocacy of women's rights based on the equality of the sexes. The Women's Movement has always fought and stood for the empowerment of women in the workplace and for social, financial, legislative, and cultural equality. The roles of women changed as they began to enter the workforce and demand equal rights.

Women's liberation moved into the home where followers of the movement challenged the traditional role of the wife. As feminism grew, more women opposed their domestic roles and submission to the husband as their authority, biblical or otherwise. Feminists chose to embrace an un-biblical view regarding a wife's position and role in marriage. Women are still advocating for rights and equality as other movements for the advancement and protection of women are in progress.

The role of a wife from a biblical perspective does not meet the objectives of the Women's Liberation Movement, which is to free women of all male authority in a male-dominated society, make them equal, give them complete autonomy and control over their lives and bodies.

Although the battle for women's equality is a worthy pursuit, it must not conflict with the role God has ordained for the Christian wife. God requires a wife to submit to her husband and has given the husband the God-ordained role has her authority. God also empowered wives to do his will through the power of the Holy Spirit. To *empower* means to give authority and power, to give permission and enable one to fulfill a specific task. God has empowered the Christian wife with authority and ability to carry out her role in accordance with his word.

> For God is working in you, giving you the desire and the power to do what pleases him.[2]

The World's View of Submission:

Some women have been misinformed or deceived about a wife's biblical role of submission, or they have been mistreated under a worldly and un-biblical form of submission. A secular view of submission is that it is self-abasing, self-humiliating, and oppressive, suggesting domination, cruelty, and persecution. The Women's Movement believes that submission is a result of a male-dominated society. They believe that "men have an authority and legitimacy only by virtue of being male."[3] They believe any authority a man has over a woman, even in the home, is a result of male supremacy, not God-ordained authority.

1. What role, if any, do you think feminism should play in a Christian marriage? _____
   _____
   _____

2. Do you think submission takes away the rights of a wife? Why or why not? _____
   _____
   _____

The Biblical View of a Wife's Role:

Many wives, including Christian wives, do not understand their biblical role. If they do understand it, they choose not to embrace it. Some women believe being under authority of any kind or being designated to a role in marriage is a violation of rights. Unaware of God's complete sovereignty over their lives, they have been deceived into believing they can attain their desire to be self-sufficient, self-ruled, and self-willed.

2. Philippians 2:13 (NLT2)
3. National Women's Liberation, "What We Want"

In the Garden of Eden, Eve was also deceived by Satan into believing she could control her own life. Genesis chapter 2 gives the account of Eve's sinful desires.

> But the serpent said to the woman, "You will not surely die. For God knows that when you eat of it your eyes will be opened, and you will be like God, knowing good and evil." So, when the woman saw that the tree was good for food, and that it was a delight to the eyes, and that the tree was to be desired to make one wise . . .» she took of its fruit and ate, and she also gave some to her husband who was with her, and he ate. Then the eyes of both were opened, and they knew that they were naked. And they sewed fig leaves together and made themselves loincloths.[4]

1. Eve desired self-sufficiency: how was Eve deceived by the false promise of self-sufficiency because of her sinful desire to be autonomous and independent of God? _____
   _____
   _____

2. Eve desired self-rule: God's command to Adam and Eve was, "You may surely eat of every tree of the garden, but of the tree of the knowledge of good and evil you shall not eat."[5] Eve was no doubt aware of this command when she told the serpent, "God said."[6] According to Genesis 3:6a, how did Eve choose self-rule and disobey God's command? _____
   _____
   _____

3. Eve desired self-will: She exercised self-will against God's will, "for in the day that you eat of it you shall surely die."[7] God's will for Adam and Eve was to live forever in paradise, getting to know him and his works.[8] According to Genesis 3:6b, how did Eve choose self-will against God's will? _____
   _____
   _____

4. Genesis 3:4–7 (NASB)
5. Genesis 2:17a (NASB)
6. Genesis 3:3 (NASB)
7. Genesis 2:17b (NASB)
8. Psalms 115:16; Ecclesiastes 3:10–11 (NASB)

Adam and Eve's sin caused the fall of man from their perfect environment in the Garden, but God's plan of redemption through Christ reverses the curse and justifies us into a right relationship with God.

A wife who refuses to embrace God's word as it relates to her role as a wife needs to understand that her rebellion is a desire for self-rule and self-will. She has been deceived into believing that she can be self-sufficient.

Read the Scriptures in the tables below and pray them back to God. Journal how God has answered your prayers and how his word encouraged you to surrender to him. Commit to turn from a self-oriented life and live according to God's word in your marriage.

Self-ruled:	Surrenders to God's authority:
Disobedient to God's word.	Submits to God in obedience.[9]
Ruled by lust and passions.	God rules her heart.[10]
Feelings of entitlement.	Relies only on God's grace.[11]
Rejects authority.	Submits to authority.[12]
Worships control.	Worships Christ as Lord of her life.[13]
Self-willed:	**Surrenders to God's will:**
Does what pleases self.	Obedient to God's will.[14]
Selfish ambition.	Considers others more important than herself.[15]

9. Romans 6:17; James 4:7 (NASB)
10. 1 Kings 8:61; John 4:23–24 (NASB)
11. 1 Corinthians 15:10; Romans 12:3 (NASB)
12. Ephesians 5:22; Colossians 3:18; 1 Peter 2:13 (NASB)
13. Acts 2:23; 1 Peter 3:15 (NASB)
14. Luke 22:42; John 5:30 (NASB)
15. Philippians 2:3 (NASB)

Ruled by lust and passions.	Denies self.[16]
Worships pleasure.	Self-controlled.[17]
Deception of self-sufficiency:	**Surrenders to God's sufficiency:**
Credits self for success.	Acknowledges God's grace.[18]
Low view of God.	A proper view of God.[19]
A high view of self.	A proper view of self.[20]
Ruled by pride.	Humbled by God's grace.[21]
Worships independence.	Dependence on God alone.[22]

The Role of the Wife:

What is the wife's role according to God's word? Be a fitting helper to her husband:

> Then the Lord God said, "It is not good that the man should be alone; I will make him a helper fit for him."[23]

> The man gave names to all livestock and the birds of the heavens and every beast of the field. But for Adam, there was not found a helper fit for him. So, the lord God caused a deep sleep to fall upon the man, and while he slept took one of his ribs and closed up its

16. Matthew 16:24; Mark 8:34 (NASB)
17. Titus 2:12; Galatians 5:23–24 (NASB)
18. Philippians 2:12–13 (NASB)
19. John 15:5; Romans 11:36 (NASB)
20. Ephesians 2:1–10; Romans 12:3 (NASB)
21. 1 Corinthians 15:10 (NASB)
22. 2 Corinthians 3:5; Colossians 1:29; Psalms 123:2 (NASB)
23. Genesis 2:18 (NASB)

place with flesh. And the rib that the lord God had taken from the man he made into a woman and brought her to the man.[24]

Eve was created to solve the problem of loneliness for Adam. Every creature that God made had a fitting mate except for Adam. God knew how to resolve the issue he saw for Adam, even if Adam was unaware of what was missing.

The wife's role is to fulfill the needs, deficiencies, and insufficiencies of the husband. She does that by helping him in any area needed to support and encourage him as he takes his place as head of the home.

A wife who is a fitting helper advances the goals and plans of her husband by supporting his decisions. She undergirds (strengthens or reinforces) his decisions and efforts through prayer. She submits and cooperates with the direction he chooses to lead her and the family.

The Excellent and Fitting Wife of Proverbs 31:

The Proverbs 31 wife is a personification of a godly, noble wife. You may never fully achieve all the attributes of a perfect wife, as depicted in Proverbs 31, but she is someone who you can aspired to. Her help, service, charity, wisdom, practicality, and ingenuity make her a fitting helper to her husband. Scripture is careful to say that she was held in high honor by her husband and esteemed by her children.

As you read through Proverbs 31:10–30, take note of the following characteristics of an excellent wife:

- Her husband safely trusts in her (v. 11).

- Her ingenuity adds value to him (v. 11).

- She is a benefit, not a detriment (v. 12).

- She makes practical purchases and finds bargains (v.14).

- She buys a property and makes investments (v.16).

- She elevates her husband because of her reputation (v. 23).

- She is a profitable entrepreneur (v. 24).

- She is a wise teacher (v. 26).

- She is the manager of her home (v. 27).

24. Genesis 2:20–22 (NASB)

1. If you were to hire an assistant at home or work, list of all the qualities you would want from that person: _____

_____

_____

2. What skills, talents, attributes, or qualities do you have that would make you a fitting helper to your husband? _____

_____

_____

    Your wife will be like a fruitful vine within your house; your children will be like olive shoots around your table.[25]

    A wife who is a fitting helper is:

- Fruitful.
- Trustworthy.
- Industrious.
- A supporter.
- Manages the home.
- Makes the home a peaceful place of rest.

1. Is there an example of a woman in your life, or someone you admire, that exemplifies a fitting helper and fruitful vine who was or is an encouraging, helpful, kind, prayerful, thriving force in the home? _____

_____

_____

2. List some of her attributes and qualities and what you could learn from her:

25. Psalms 128:3 (ESV)

Her attributes and qualities:	What you can learn from her:

The role of the wife: Submit to your husband's authority.

Counseling Issue:

Anna was a self-ruled wife who was convinced that her husband insisting she cook was a "power play" and an attempt to "lord over her." Anna believed that she had the right to cook when she chose to and felt that her husband should respect that right. His insistence that she prepares meals seemed more to Anna as a way for her husband to exploit his authority. Refusing to cook was only a symptom of a bigger problem of refusing to submit to God-ordained authority and ultimately to God.[26]

It is essential that wives know and embrace the biblical truth about submission. Only by knowing what God says about submission will a wife be willing and able to bring herself under submission with joy. She can anticipate what God will do for wives who are obedient to his word: "Blessed rather are these who hear the word of God and obey it."[27] Only through God's word, the work of the spirit, and encouragement from other believers can a wife be sanctified to serve God and to serve her husband.[28]

First, let's clear up some misconceptions about biblical submission: biblical submission does not mean that the wife is inferior to her husband.

> Husbands love your wives, just as Christ loved the church and gave Himself up for her.[29]

26. James 4:7; Colossians 3:18; 1 Peter 2:13 (NASB)
27. Luke 11:28 (NASB)
28. John 17:17 (NASB)
29. Ephesians 5:25 (NASB)

God requires a husband to love his wife as Christ himself loved the church. Christ loved the church so much he gave himself up for her. This sacrificial kind of love puts the other first. This sacrificial love indicates that wives are to be held in the highest regard, with honor and as someone worth the sacrifice.

Likewise, husbands live with your wives in an understanding way, showing honor to the woman as the weaker vessel, since they are heirs with you of the grace of life, so that your prayers may not be hindered.[30]

The Bible says that a husband must elevate his wife as someone worthy to be honored, treated with special care (like delicate china), and treated as one who is an equal heir to all God's graces and eternal life.[31]

1. Why is it important for a wife to know and embrace what God says about submission? _____

_____

_____

2. What does a sacrificial kind of love look like? _____

_____

_____

> Biblical submission does not mean that the wife has no opinion, makes no decisions, or that she should remain silent.

The virtuous wife of Proverbs 31:10–31 was an industrious business-woman. She made decisions about her business and her household. A wife adds value and experience to the marriage. She can be a help to her husband in many ways and serve many functions. A wife's opinions and ideas add value to the home. Her gifts, talents, and experience can help her husband make wise decisions and be used for the benefit of the home, for others, and for the glory of God. Although the husband is the head of the household, the wife can take charge of any task that utilizes the gifts, skills, and opportunities God has given her.

As leader of the home, how can your husband benefit from your gifts, talents and experience? _____

_____

_____

30. 1 Peter 3:7 (NASB)
31. 1 Peter 3:7 (NASB)

> Biblical submission does not mean a wife must take the wheel when a husband is passive.

Wives may believe that they must take control if their husband is passive and fails to take the lead within the home. They may even make the mistake of thinking their husband's silence and docile personality permits them to assume his role as a leader.

The Counseling Issue:

Kara, a self-willed wife, interpreted her husband's lack of response as a green light to do what she wanted. His passivity gave her the opportunity to make all the decisions. Kara usurped her husband's role as head of the home without any apparent opposition. It soon became clear that her husband had emotionally and physically separated from their marriage relationship. His failure to lead gave liberty for Kara to take control. Kara used this liberty as an opportunity to seek her fleshly desires.

Adam's lack of response in the garden allowed Eve to usurp Adam's authority in disobedience to God.[32] Adam's passivity ("because you listened to your wife"[33]) allowed Eve's self-will to lead them into disobedience. A wife who desires and insists on forcing her own will and taking control cannot expect that a passive husband will take the lead until she lines up under her proper role of submission.

The wife must forsake her desire to control and lead her husband and her home. She has to hand over the authority to him to lead, whether he wants it or not. One problem may be that when he tries to lead, the wife criticizes his decisions and belittles him when he makes mistakes. Because of his fear of failure, being ridiculed, and having to take the blame, he abdicates his role as a leader to his judgmental wife.

Read Genesis Chapter 3: In Genesis 3:16, the word "desire" in this passage and in Genesis 4:7 means to rule.

Because Adam's sin was credited to us, we are hard-wired to desire to control our husbands. However, Jesus's sacrifice on the cross bought us justification and saved us from the grip of our desires into a righteous relationship with the Lord.

---

32. Genesis 3:6 (NASB)

33. Genesis 3:17 (NASB)

Therefore, just as sin entered the world through one man, and death through sin, so also death was passed on to all men, because all sinned.[34] But the gift is not like the trespass. For if the many died by the trespass of the one man, how much more did God's grace and the gift that came by the grace of the one man, Jesus Christ, abound to the many![35]

> For sin shall not be your master, because you are not under law, but under grace.[36]

1. In what ways can a wife get in the way of her husband's attempts to lead? _____
_____
_____

2. What must a wife do to encourage a passive husband to take the lead in the home? _____
_____
_____

3. What is the driving force behind a wife's desire to take control over her husband and her home? _____
_____
_____

4. What saves a wife from yielding to this destructive desire against God's will? _____
_____
_____

> Biblical submission does not mean a husband's sin disqualifies him to lead.

A wife may believe that a husband who falls into sin is disqualified from leading her. Although her trust in him may be tested, she cannot use his sins against him to usurp his leadership and take control or threaten to leave if she cannot have her way. If she does, she becomes the judge and jury

34. Romans 5: 12 (NASB)
35. Romans 5:15 (NASB)
36. Romans 6:14 (NASB)

and fails to rely on God's mercy, the promise of forgiveness, and his plan to perfect them both through this adversity.[37]

> Likewise, wives, be subject to your own husbands, so that even if some do not obey the word, they may be won without a word by the conduct of their wives, when they see your respectful and pure conduct.[38]

The word "likewise" means in the same way. One should submit to the authority of all human institutions and leaders as mentioned in 1 Peter 2:13–25.

God's command is clear that wives must submit, even when a spouse is in sin. Serving a husband in humility and submission is a way to win him "without a word." There is no cancellation clause for submission to a sinning spouse.

List the misconceptions that some believe about biblical submission. Or list the reasons a wife may give for not submitting to her husband:

1. _____
   _____

2. _____
   _____

3. _____
   _____

4. _____
   _____

Are there any areas, situations, or circumstances where you find it hard to submit; why? _____
_____
_____

37. James 1:1–4, 2:13, 4:11–12 (NASB)

38. 1 Peter 3:1–2

What does it mean to submit to a husband's authority?

- Biblical submission is a command from an absolutely just and absolutely righteous God who loved us first. In contrast, worldly submission may be thought of as capitulation under an unfair, self-serving dictatorship.

- Servanthood is a defining characteristic of submission, and it is also a characteristic of Christ. Christ served in humility when he washed his disciple's feet.[39] Christ also chose the greatest act of humility by offering himself as a sacrifice for humanity.

- Biblical submission is an act of servanthood that a wife is compelled to place herself under because of the sacrifice Christ made for her. If a wife is a faithful follower of Jesus, submission is an acceptable form of subjection for the sake of Christ.

Why Should you Submit to Your Husband?

Christ demonstrated submission to the Father.

Read the following the Scripture and write down how Christ submitted to the Father:

1. He went away again a second time and prayed, saying, "My Father, if this cup cannot pass away unless I drink it, Your will be done."[40] _____
   _____
   _____

2. "For I have come down from heaven, not to do My own will, but the will of Him who sent Me."[41] _____
   _____
   _____

39. Luke 7:44 (NASB)
40. Matthew 26:42 (NASB)
41. John 6:38 (NASB)

3. "When all things are subjected to Him, then the Son Himself also will be subjected to the One who subjected all things to Him, so that God may be all in all."[42] _____

    _____

    _____

4. "Have this attitude in yourselves which was also in Christ Jesus, who, although He existed in the form of God, did not regard equality with God a thing to be grasped, but emptied Himself, taking the form of a bond-servant, *and* being made in the likeness of men. Being found in appearance as a man, He humbled Himself by becoming obedient to the point of death, even death on a cross. For this reason also, God highly exalted Him, and bestowed on Him the name which is above every name"[43] _____

    _____

    _____

> Submission is a direct command from God because it is a reflection of the image of Christ

Several times in Scripture, God gives a direct command for wives to submit to their husbands.

Read the following Scriptures and write down what each says about the wife's responsibility to submit:

1. "Wives, *be subject* to your own husbands, as to the Lord. For the husband is the head of the wife, as Christ also is the head of the church, He Himself *being* the Savior of the body. But as the church is subject to Christ, so also the wives *ought to be* to their husbands in everything."[44]

    _____

    _____

2. "Wives, submit to your husbands, as is fitting in the Lord."[45] ___ ___

    _____

    _____

---

42. 1 Corinthians 15:28 (NASB)
43. Philippians 2:5–9 (NASB)
44. Ephesians 5:22–24 (NASB)
45. Colossians 3:18 (NASB)

3. "Likewise, wives, be subject to your own husbands, so that even if some do not obey the word, they may be won without a word by the conduct of their wives"[46] _____

_____

_____

4. "so that they may encourage the young women to love their husbands, to love their children, *to be* sensible, pure, workers at home, kind, being subject to their own husbands, so that the word of God will not be dishonored."[47] _____

_____

_____

If submission is a direct command from a just and righteous God, what are some possible reasons a Christian wife would choose not to embrace it? __

_____

_____

Submission is for the Wife's Good:

Submission is ordained for the wife's protection and covering. When a wife embraces this truth, she can be confident that God will be a strong tower and a refuge. When we place ourselves under God-ordained authorities, God will bless our obedience and provide protection.

Submission is freedom from bearing the responsibilities of leadership. Leadership requires carrying others' burdens and sacrifices. A leader's concern is to meet the needs of others. He must be willing to sacrifice himself—his personal needs, wants, desires, aspirations, time, money. The needs of others are more important than his own.

Submission is God's Creative Plan and Purpose:

God created man and woman equally but with unique and distinctive roles. God could have created man and woman in the same manner. Scripture is clear that the roles of men and women are distinct, and that man is the head

46. 1 Peter 3:1 (NASB)

47. Titus 2:4–5 (NASB)

of the woman: "For the husband is the head of the wife, as Christ also is the head of the church, He Himself being the Savior of the body."[48] Men are called to lead the home and the church with a sacrificial, spiritual leadership. Women are called to respect, embrace, and submit to that leadership whether it is spiritual or not, except for submitting to sin.

> For Adam was formed first, then Eve[49]

> For man was not made from woman, but woman from man. Neither was man created for woman, but woman for man[50]

> Wives, submit to your own husbands, as to the Lord. For the husband is the head of the wife even as Christ is the head of the church, his body, and is himself its Savior. Now as the church submits to Christ, so also wives should submit in everything to their husbands[51]

> But Peter and the other apostles replied, "We must obey God rather than men."[52]

Submission is a Willful Choice:

Wives must bring themselves under submission willfully.[53] They can be forced to obey but not to have a heart of submission.[54]

Wives cannot be shamed, humiliated, or dragged into submission. It is a deliberate choice in response to our desire to please God and be like Christ.[55] It is also a result of a spirit-filled life to desire to do God's will. If a wife does not make a willful choice to submit, then any submission she show is likely an attempt to manipulate her husband or it is a submission out of fear of her husband—her heart does not embrace submission out of humble obedience to God.

48. Ephesians 5:23 (NASB)

49. 1 Timothy 2:13 (NASB)

50. 1 Corinthians 11:8–9 (NASB)

51. Ephesians 5:23 (NASB)

52. Acts 5:29 (NASB)

53. Ephesians 5:22; 1 Peter 3:1 (NASB)

54. Psalms 40:7–8 (NASB)

55. John 6:38, 8:29 (NASB)

But Peter and John replied, "Judge for yourselves whether it is right in God's sight to listen to you rather than God."[56]

What is the one exception to submitting to a husband? _____

_____

_____

Biblical Submission Removes Fear:

Biblical submission removes a wife's fear because she is ultimately placing herself under the subjection of the Lord and the safety of his will. It eliminates the fear of misuse of authority because God promises he can move on behalf of those under authority, even harsh authority.

> Take my yoke upon you, and learn from me, for I am gentle and lowly in heart, and you will find rest for your souls. For my yoke is easy, and my burden is light.[57]

> Let every person be subject to the governing authorities. For there is no authority except from God, and those that exist have been instituted by God.[58]

> The king's heart is a stream of water in the hand of the lord; he turns it wherever he will.[59]

Biblical submission removes fear of a husband's weaknesses and sins. Abigail's humility saved her entire household from death because of her foolish husband Nabal.[60]

The Bible encourages wives married to unbelieving husbands to keep doing what is right before the Lord as holy women, not from fear or force, but from a desire to please God.[61]

1. What fears do you have about submitting to a husband's authority? __

_____

_____

56. Acts. 4:18 (NASB)

57. Matthew 11:29–30 (ESV)

58. Romans 13:1 (NASB)

59. Proverbs 21:1 (NASB)

60. 1 Samuel 25 (NASB)

61. 1 Peter 3:1–6 (NASB)

2. When a wife chooses to willfully submit to her husband, whose subjection and authority is she ultimately under? _____

_____

_____

3. Why is being under submission a safe place to be? _____

_____

_____

There is no cancellation clause for submission to a husband who is foolish or unsaved.[62] A wife should not submit if her husband asks her to sin, nor should she follow her husband into sin.[63] A wife may be tempted to be fearful if she chooses not to follow her husband's sins and chooses instead to follow God in obedience. She must trust that God will bless her choice to remain faithful to him.

The Role of the Wife:

Respect the husband's position.

> However, let each one of you love his wife as himself, and let the wife see that she respects her husband.[64]

A wife can love her husband without respecting him if she loves him only for what he does for her. This love is conditional. A wife can love her husband without respecting him if he is willing to give her control. This wife is usually self-ruled, self-willed, and believes she is self-sufficient.

Respecting a husband's position means respecting the God-ordained role that he has been given by an absolutely righteous and just God.

What Keeps a Wife from Respecting her Husband?

A wife will not respect her husband's position if she opposes God's sovereign right and all-knowing wisdom to give the man authority over the wife.

If a wife is self-ruled and rejects God's rule over her life, then she will not embrace God's authority or her husband's authority in the home.

---

62. 1 Peter 3:3–6 (NASB)
63. Acts 5:29 (NASB)
64. Ephesians 5:33 (NASB)

The Truth:

The husband is to be respected regardless of his spiritual condition. If he is unsaved, he is due respect and reverence from his wife.

Even if a wife is more educated, more gifted, makes more money, believes she is smarter, or comes from an affluent or wealthy lineage, she is to submit and respect her husband's position.

A respectful wife will show love and encouragement even when she is disappointed by the husband's choices and failures. A husband's weaknesses can compel a wife to grumble and complain. This response reveals a lack of respect.

> The wise woman builds her house, But the foolish tears it down with her own hands.[65]

What does Proverbs 14:1 look like in practice as it relates to respect? _____
_____
_____

Responses That Reveal A Lack of Respect Toward Your Husband:

Tearing Down:

- Lack of confidence in his decisions. An expectation of failure when he makes decisions you do not agree with.
- Being defensive or reactionary to his decisions.
- Being unappreciative and critical of his efforts because they were not done your way.
- Belittling him in front of others or making jokes at his expense.
- Constant battering and nagging.
- Interrogating him about his reasons or choices he has decided to make or has made.
- Opposing him and arguing with him in front of children, others, or on social media.

65. Proverbs 14:1 (NASB)

- Communicating with him in a parent-to-child style of communication; "You need to . . . ," "I told you to . . ."

- Condescending and disapproving body language and gestures.

- Intolerance of his shortcomings and errors. Holding grudges and keeping a record of all his wrongs.

Responses That Reveal Submission and Respect Toward Your Husband:

Building Up:

- Confidence in his decisions. A prayerful expectation that God will guide his decisions.

- Getting onboard with his decisions.

- Appreciating his efforts even if they are not done when and how you want them.[66]

- Holding him in honor and respect in front of others at all times.[67]

- Being loving, patient, and tolerant even when he procrastinates. Continuing to nag about a matter only drives him away.[68]

- Asking if he will share the reasons he made certain decisions and discuss things openly and lovingly with forbearance. Give your full support to his choices.[69]

- Deal with differences in private, choosing the right time and place, in humility and open-mindedness.[70]

- Communicate respectfully without demands, threats, profanity, or superiority—not as a parent or teacher.[71]

- Unspoken words and actions are no less disrespectful.[72]

66. 1 Corinthians 13:4–5 (NASB)
67. Ephesians 5:33 (NASB)
68. Proverbs 21 9:19, 19:13, 25:24, 27:15 (NASB)
69. Ephesians 4:2, 31–32; Colossians 3:12–14; Proverbs 31:26 (NASB)
70. Proverbs 15:23; Colossians 3:12–13 (NASB)
71. Ephesians 4:29; Ecclesiastes 10:12 (NASB)
72. 1 Thessalonians 5:11; Romans 13:14 (NASB)

A man's greatest need is respect. Lack of submission and respect is a direct assault against a husband's leadership in the home. Lack of respect disrupts unity, destroys intimacy, and corrupts communication.

If a husband is denied his leadership in the home, he may compensate by sinfully holding back in other areas in which he does have control: his affection, his compassion, his compromise, and his communication. Scripture reminds us that a wise wife builds her house, but a foolish one tears hers down by her own hands.[73]

Read the following Scriptures and answer the corresponding questions:

1. "Wives submit to your own husbands, as to the Lord."[74] In what ways can you subject yourself to your husband's authority, honoring his position in the same way the church subjects herself to Christ? _____

_____

_____

2. "Likewise, wives, be subject to your own husbands, so that even if some do not obey the word, they may be won without a word by the conduct of their wives, when they see your respectful and pure conduct."[75] According to 1 Peter 3:1–2, if you are required to submit to your husband's God-ordained position, how much does your husband's spiritually, personality flaws or weaknesses matter regarding your level of submission? _____

_____

_____

3. In what ways does willful and joyful submission to your husband make you more like Christ? _____

_____

_____

Conclusion:

The purpose of this section is to correct the misconceptions and explain the truths about the biblical role of a wife. By clearly defining the wife's role and what it looks like in practice, our prayer is that you will

73. Proverbs 14:1 (NASB)

74. Ephesians 5:22 (ESV)

75. 1 Peter 3:1–2 (ESV)

be encouraged to fulfill your role as an act of worship to God. You will receive the blessings of obedience, produce unity, peace, and harmony in your marriage and your home.

Overview:

What is the wife's role according to God's word?

Be a Fitting Helper to her Husband:

> Then the Lord God said, "It is not good that the man should be alone; I will make him a helper fit for him."[76]

Submit to her Husband's Authority:

Submission is a direct command from God. Several times in Scripture, God gives a direct command for wives to submit to their husbands:

- "Wives be subject to your own husband, as to the Lord."[77]
- "For the husband is the head of the wife, as Christ also is the head of the church, He Himself being the Savior of the body."[78]
- "Wives, submit to your husbands, as is fitting in the Lord."[79]
- "Likewise, wives, be subject to your own husbands, so that even if some do not obey the word, they may be won without a word by the conduct of their wives."[80]

- Submission is for the wife's good.
- Submission is God's creative plan and purpose.
- Submission is a willful choice.
- Biblical submission removes fear.

76. Genesis 2:18 (NASB)
77. Ephesians 5:22 (NASB)
78. Ephesians 5:23 (NASB)
79. Colossians 3:18 (NASB)
80. 1 Peter 3:1 (NASB)

Respect her Husband's Position:

However, let each one of you love his wife as himself, and let the wife see that she respects her husband.[81]

---

81. Ephesians 5:33 (NASB)

4

Differences, Expectations, and Preferences

Counseling Issue:

JOANN IS EMOTIONALLY SENSITIVE when it comes to dealing with unfavorable situations, circumstances, and events. Dave seems to maintain a calm composure, even in the most challenging conditions. Joann views Dave's mild response to stressful situations as a lack of concern for real problems. She accuses Dave of not caring because of his apparent lack of emotions. Dave assures her that he does care. However, he accuses Joann of being too emotional and overreacting to small things. He says she makes a big deal out of nothing.

Joann is a social butterfly—she is the life of the party. Dave, on the other hand, enjoys spending time alone and is not that interested in going to social events. Joann expects Dave to take her out regularly, but she complains that all Dave wants to do is sit at home on the computer or watch TV. Dave claims they do more than enough activities together; he believes that if Joann would cook more often, they could have dinner at home and spend time together alone.

When it comes to home repairs, Dave usually finds a maintenance specialist, and if he feels the price is reasonable, he schedules a time to get the repair done. But Joann believes that Dave should get several estimates first before paying for repairs. Dave's mindset is, "let's just get it done," while Joann likes "considering all the options."

The Common Problem:

Differences, expectations, and preferences.

The Common Result:

Frustration, conflict, and disunity.

Objective:

The purpose of the chapter is to help couples understand how their differences, unmet expectations, and personal preferences can hinder or enhance their relationship.

Too many couples come into the relationship struggling because they allow personal preferences to take precedence over their relationship. Many of them end up frustrated and disappointed. To overcome this, couples must learn the importance of grace and acceptance. In doing so, they will grow to appreciate their differences, eliminate unrealistic expectations, and avoid the temptation of allowing personal preferences to cause disunity in their relationship. They will learn to love one another in a way that pleases God and maintains oneness, despite differences, expectations, and preferences. They will come to realize that their differences are by God's divine design.

The Significance of Differences:

Genesis 1:26–27 says, "God created man in His own image, in the image of God He created him; male and female He created them."

According to Genesis 1:27, male and female were created differently. In what ways are males and females different?

1. Physically: _____

_____

_____

2. Emotionally: _____

_____

_____

3. Mentally (how we think): _____

    _____

    _____

4. Communication (concrete: direct and to the point; or abstract: the need to involve details): _____

    _____

    _____

Now let's read 1 Corinthians 12:12–18:

> But the same Spirit works all these things, distributing to each one individually just as He wills. For even as the body is one and *yet* has many members, and all the members of the body, though they are many, are one body, so also is Christ. For by one Spirit we were all baptized into one body, whether Jews or Greeks, whether slaves or free, and we were all made to drink of one Spirit. For the body is not one member, but many. If the foot says, "Because I am not a hand, I am not *a part* of the body," it is not for this reason any the less *a part* of the body. And if the ear says, "Because I am not an eye, I am not *a part* of the body," it is not for this reason any the less *a part* of the body. If the whole body were an eye, where would the hearing be? If the whole were hearing, where would the sense of smell be? But now God has placed the members, each one of them, in the body, just as He desired.

1. What does this passage say about differences? _____

    _____

    _____

2. How are you and your mate similar? _____

    _____

    _____

3. How are you and your mate different? _____

    _____

    _____

4. Which of your differences seem the most problematic? In other words, do you find some of your differences irritating? Explain: _____

    _____

    _____

5. Are differences a cause for conflict? _____

_____

_____

6. From a biblical perspective, how should you respond to your differences? _____

_____

_____

> And if one member suffers, all the members suffer with it; if *one* member is honored, all the members rejoice with it.[1]

7. You and your spouse are different but yet you are two people striving to live as one flesh. How does 1 Corinthians 12:26 relate to marriage?

_____

_____

Point:

Some problems occur in marriages because of an unwillingness to accept differences, but husbands and wives were created differently by God's design. As such, your goal is not to get your spouse to think, feel, and communicate the way you do. Differences do not have to be an occasion for conflict. Differences create occasions for conflict—they are not the cause (to be discussed later). Your differences can complement each other, add richness and depth to your marriage, and provide an opportunity to expand your thinking.

What Do You Expect from Your Mate?

> Hope deferred makes the heart sick, But desire fulfilled is a tree of life.[2]

1. 1 Corinthians 12:26 (NASB)
2. Proverbs 13:12 (NASB)

Definition:

Expectation: to look forward to; regard as likely to happen, to anticipate.

What do you want, need, or desire from your mate? What are some things you hope for or anticipate receiving from your spouse? List them on the chart below (Examples: Cooking, cleaning, making repairs, financial stability, etc.):

What I Expect from My Spouse:

Some expectations can be good, bad, reasonable, unreasonable, realistic, or unrealistic. Nevertheless, Scriptures says that, "Hope [expectations] deferred makes the heart sick, But desire fulfilled is a tree of life."[3]

1. What does it feel like when your spouse fails to meet some of the expectations you listed on the chart? _____
   _____
   _____

2. In what ways do unmet expectations make the heart sick? _____
   _____

3. How do you typically respond when your mate fails to meet your expectations regarding things that you hope for, want, need, and desire?
   _____
   _____

3. Proverbs 13:12 (NASB)

4. Are the expectations you have for your spouse realistic? Why or why not? _____

_____

_____

5. Do you believe your mate's expectations of you are unrealistic? Please explain: _____

_____

_____

Read the following Scripture about trust:

> Thus says the lord, "Cursed is the man who trusts in mankind And makes flesh his strength, And whose heart turns away from the lord. For he will be like a bush in the desert And will not see when prosperity comes, But will live in stony wastes in the wilderness, A land of salt without inhabitant. Blessed is the man who trusts in the lord And whose trust is the lord. For he will be like a tree planted by the water, That extends its roots by a stream And will not fear when the heat comes; But its leaves will be green, And it will not be anxious in a year of drought Nor cease to yield fruit. The heart is more deceitful than all else And is desperately sick; Who can understand it?"[4]

1. According to Jeremiah 17:5–6, what are the consequences of placing your trust in yourself and in man? _____

_____

_____

2. According to Jeremiah 17:7–8, what are the consequences of placing your trust in the Lord? _____

_____

_____

3. What is the relationship between trust and expectations? _____

_____

_____

4. In consideration of Jeremiah 17:9, what's wrong with our hearts and can our hearts be trusted? _____

_____

_____

4. Jeremiah 17:5–9 (NASB)

The Reality of Expectations:

- You can expect problems in marriage.
- You can anticipate conflict because you will not always see things the same way.
- You can expect disappointment.
- You cannot place your trust in man because man will let you down.
- The fact is, you cannot always trust yourself—we all fall short.

There is one thing you cannot always expect: You cannot always expect your spouse to give you everything you hope for, want, need, or desire. He or she will fall short and miss the mark. And so will you. Why? Because you are both sinners who said "I do" in marriage. You are both a work in progress.

Point:

The truth is, the word of God is our only source of expectations available to us that is pure and true. We can expect that God is a god who keeps his promises. Blessed are those who put their trust in the Lord.

What About Personal Preferences?

Reminder:

An expectation is what you want or anticipate, and preference has to do with how you expect to receive it.

Preferences:

Preferring one way or thing over another; something that you have a liking for; what you believe is logical, practical, or ideal. In essence, expressing a preference is equivalent to expressing an opinion.

Two Responses to Unmet Expectations and Preferences:

- With tranquility: forbearance: grace, mercy, patience, restraint, endurance, living with it.
- With turbulence: clear sin: angry, bitter, resentment, retaliation, blowing up, shutting down, avoidance.

1. How do you respond when your mate does not do things according to your preferences or when he or she refuses to do things according to the way you believe they should be done? _____
   _____
   _____

Philippians 2:3–4 says, "Do nothing from selfishness or empty conceit, but with humility of mind regard one another as more important than yourselves; do not *merely* look out for your own personal interests, but also for the interests of others."

2. According to Philippians 2:3, what compels a person only to be concerned about their own opinion? _____
   _____
   _____

> He who separates himself seeks *his own* desire, He quarrels against all sound wisdom. A fool does not delight in understanding, But only in revealing his own mind.[5]

3. What does Proverbs 18:1–2 say about a person who is only concerned about their own opinion or personal preference? _____
   _____
   _____

According to Proverbs 18:1–2, a person who is only concerned about himself:

- Separates himself from others by seeing himself as better or smarter than others. His way is not just the right way, but it is the only way.
- Is only concerned about what he wants.

5. Proverbs 18:1–2 (NASB)

- Fights against those who confront him with the truth.
- Does not take pleasure in understanding what others have to say, because he believes the only opinion that matters is his own.

The Bible calls this kind of a person a F_____.

What is the proper response to preferences/opinions?

Do nothing from selfishness or empty conceit, but with humility of mind regard one another as more important than yourselves; do not *merely* look out for your own personal interests, but also for the interests of others.[6]

In the Backdrop of Philippians 2:3–4:

1. How should a wife respond when her husband requests her to do something when and how he prefers it to be done? _____
   _____
   _____

2. What must a husband remember as he shares his preferences with his wife? _____
   _____
   _____

Point:

Not all arguments that couples have are blatant sin issues and offenses. The truth is many arguments among married couples are more about personal preferences and opinions than they are about sin issues.

Conclusion:

Standing together despite differences and personal preferences prevents you from being torn apart. Scripture says differences can be complimentary.

6. Philippians 2:3–4 (NASB)

There are advantages to being different.[7] There is also strength in maintaining unity despite differences, expectations, and preferences. Scripture says,

> Two are better than one because they have a good return for their labor. For if either of them falls, the one will lift up his companion. But woe to the one who falls when there is not another to lift him up. Furthermore, if two lie down together they keep warm, but how can one be warm *alone?* And if one can overpower him who is alone, two can resist him. A cord of three *strands* is not quickly torn apart.[8]

Ecclesiastes 4:9–12 was written in the context of someone who is preparing for battle. It is a battle plan of victory over the enemy. The truth is that marriages are under attack by Satan. Because the marriage relationship reflects Christ and the church, Satan wants to destroy the marriage made in the image of God. If Satan is successful at destroying marriages, he can succeed in destroying families and then the church.

Sometimes a spouse can stand alone and rebuke the Devil in an attempt to save the marriage. The husband or wife may refuse to stand with their spouse. A spouse who stands alone to save their marriage remains under God's protective covering and will receive God's guidance. He or she also brings glory and honor to God. When you stand to save your marriage even when the other spouse has disconnected emotionally, physically, mentally, and spiritually from the union, you will find favor with God.[9]

On the other hand, some attempt to practice individualism in their marriage. They promote their own goals and desires independent of their spouse. They also refuse to accept differences because they want to make their own decisions and have their own preferences without ever compromising. This is a person whose only concern is about self. They want what they want when they want it and how they want it. They function in the marriage without consideration of their spouse.

Problems arise when a spouse attempts to stand alone in self-sufficiency in their marriage. They see things in terms of me and mine. They elevate themselves as smarter and wiser than their spouse. From their perspective, they make better decisions than their spouse—and they know it all. When they feel opposed, they become angry and lash out against those who disagree.

7. 1 Corinthians 12:14–17 (NASB)

8. Ecclesiastes 4:9–12 (NASB)

9. 1 Peter 2:16–21 (NASB)

The reward of humility and the fear of the lord Are wealth, honor and life.[10]

Instead of having rewards for their labor, they miss out on and forfeit God's blessings upon their life. Their toil is in vain because they are attempting to labor selfishly, working against the grain of unity and harmony in the relationship. A spouse who pridefully stands alone in the marriage will eventually fall with no one to lift them up. Why wouldn't their spouse help them up? A spouse who has been resisted and rejected over time may be tempted to be reluctant to help the one who has fallen. They may sinfully take pleasure in watching the rebellious spouse suffer.

However, there is strength when a husband and wife stand together as one, even in their disagreements. They can experience power and live victoriously over situations, circumstances, and adversities. But in a marriage where a spouse stands alone in their unwillingness to accept difference, preferences, and expectations, or even to compromise, they will experience trials and could suffer losses.

Ecclesiastes 4:9–12 says two is better than one. No one can stand alone. Here is what's interesting: Most of this passage is discussing the invaluable benefits of two people standing together. However, the last verse says, "A cord of *three* strands is not quickly torn apart."

When did "two" become "three?" If two people represent two strands, then who is the third strand? The writer of Ecclesiastes makes a biblical argument that two people, especially as it relates to marriage, can stand against opposition better than one can. And three can stand stronger than two. If they are Christians, with the divine help of the Lord, then that makes a very powerful *three-strand cord* that is not easily broken, even under intense pressure or opposition. A husband and wife who stand together despite disagreements can experience blessings in their labor, the warmth and comfort of love, the power of God, and the victory of Christ. The truth is, you cannot disagree and stand in unity while maintaining unconditional love for one another apart from Christ. Christ is the third strand in the cord and strength of your marriage.

Exercise wisdom when you are relating to your spouse despite your differences, expectations, and preferences.

> But the wisdom from above is first pure, then peaceable, gentle, reasonable, full of mercy and good fruits, unwavering, without

---

10. Proverbs 22:4 (NASB)

hypocrisy. And the seed whose fruit is righteousness is sown in peace by those who make peace.[11]

"Peace cannot be kept by force. It can only be achieved by understanding."
—ALBERT EINSTEIN

1. What is the result of humility in relationships (verse 18)? _____
   _____
   _____

2. What must you have from God (from above) in order to obtain peace with your spouse? _____
   _____
   _____

3. What does wisdom from above look like in practice? _____
   _____
   _____

- It is pure: there is no selfish agenda or hidden motives.
- Peaceable: tranquil, not quarrelsome, nor a whiner, nor grumbler.
- Gentle: compassionate; tolerates being offended and response to mistreatment with kindness and gentle correction.
- Reasonable: committed to doing what is right; always ready to forgive.
- Full of mercy and good fruits: concerned about the needs of others.
- Unwavering: does not change; always concerned about fairness.
- Without hypocrisy: genuine and sincere; does not lie or put up a front.

11. James 3:17–18 (NASB)

5

Communication

Part One: Talking with Purpose

Counseling Issue:

SIMONE LIKES TO TALK and gives lots of details when she is communicating, but her husband John's communication is usually straightforward and to the point. Simone accuses John of not listening to her when she is talking. John swears that he hears her, his only problem is that Simone gives far too many details and takes too long to make her point.

In contrast, John accuses Simone of asking too many questions. John feels as if she is cross-examining him when they are engaged in casual conversation. However, Simone justifies her questioning by accusing John of failing to give enough details when he is speaking. As a result, she believes she must drag it out of him.

Furthermore, Simone accuses John of cutting her off when she is talking. John says his intent is not to cut her off. He claims he is merely responding to what Simone is saying. John says that she can be long-winded, and she sometimes expresses herself as if she is reading a dissertation and wants to treat his responses to what she has to say as endnotes. Her favorite phrase is, "Let me finish."

The Problem:

Simone and John have different styles of communicating. Simone is an abstract communicator, meaning she gives a lot of in-depth, vivid details while making her point. She wants John to experience what she is saying through her verbal picture. On the other hand, John is a concrete communicator. That is, John gets straight to the point, gives the results without providing many details. The issue is that both Simone and John want the other to communicate the way that they do. Moreover, both are only interested being heard and not listening to one another. They both desire to be understood and not seeking to understand. So, in their frustration they tear one another down with their words.

The Result:

Arguments, disunity, finger-pointing, blame-shifting, and a severe breakdown in communication. The two cannot have a decent conversation without arguing. They both fail to use words that edify one another. In the end, no one is talking, no one is listening.

How to Identify Obstacles to Effective Communications?

Purpose:

The purpose of this chapter is to help encourage and equip married couples with the biblical tools they need to identify the issues at the root of poor communication and to apply these principles so they can talk with purpose and listen for understanding. Additionally, the purpose is to correct verbal and non-verbal sin issues that hinders effective communication so that they can establish biblical oneness as God desires.

Key Scriptures:

Ephesians 4:15, 29–32, Proverbs 25:11–14

Definition: Godly Communication:

1. Using words that edify, encourage, admonish, or give wisdom, hope, and comfort to others.

2. To listen with intent for understanding, wisdom, instruction, and correction.

   You must guard your mouth against unwholesome communication.

   > Let no unwholesome word proceed from your mouth, but only such a word as is good for edification according to the need of the moment, so that it will give grace to those who hear.[1]

The word unwholesome means anything that is bad, rotten, spoiled, corrupted, worn out, and no longer fit for use. The terms "polluted" and "corrupt" are synonyms for unwholesome. When something is declared to be polluted, it is considered to be of poor quality, worthless, and unfit for human consumption. Warning signs are usually placed around bodies of water to alert fishermen that the fish in that area are considered to be unwholesome, corrupt, and polluted.

In Ephesians 4:29, the writer applies unwholesome to the words we use to communicate. Most people think of unwholesome, corrupt, or polluted communication as profanity. However, a person can avoid using profanity and say words that are still unwholesome. Consider the following examples and circle the ones that are relevant to how you communicate.

Biblical Examples of Unwholesome or Corrupt Communication:

- Talking too much and not listening.[2]
- Lying.[3]
- Cutting your spouse off while he or she is speaking.[4]
- Sarcasm.[5]

1. Ephesians 4:29 (NASB)
2. Proverbs 10:19; James 1:19 (NASB)
3. Ephesians 4:25 (NASB)
4. James 1:19 (NASB)
5. Ephesians 5:4 (NASB)

- Facial Expressions that reveal extreme displeasure or anger (rolling of the eyes, smirks, squinting).[6]

- Belittling.[7]

- Hurling Insults.[8]

- Exaggerating the facts or truth.[9]

- Misreading meaning into something your spouse said.[10]

- Becoming defensive when confronted with the truth.[11]

- Justifying your wrongs and refusing to take responsibility for your actions.[12]

- Drawing conclusions and giving an answer before hearing all the facts.[13]

- Falsely accusing someone of something they have not done.[14]

- Attempting to judge the motives of another.[15]

- Dominating conversations.[16]

- Being only concerned about your own opinion.[17]

- Being quick-tempered.[18]

- Being too critical or fault-finding.[19]

- Cursing.[20]

6. Genesis 4:5–6 (NASB)
7. Matthew 5:22 (NASB)
8. Psalms 64:3 (NASB)
9. Numbers 13:32–33 (NASB)
10. Proverbs 15:4 (NASB)
11. James 5:16 (NASB)
12. Matthew 5:23–24 (NASB)
13. Proverbs 18:13 (NASB)
14. Exodus 20:16 (NASB)
15. James 4:11–12 (NASB)
16. Proverbs 10:19 (NASB)
17. Proverbs 18:1–2; Philippians 2:4 (NASB)
18. Proverbs 15:18, 29:11; Ephesians 4:26 (NASB)
19. Pr. 11:12–13, 25:9; Matthew 18:15 (NASB)
20. Proverbs 12:18, 15:1 (NASB)

- Minimizing one's own faults and maximizing the faults of one's spouse.[21]
- Always complaining or grumbling about something.[22]
- Insisting on having things your way.[23]
- Nagging: saying the same thing repeatedly.[24]

Many times, couples ignore how they communicate and fail to realize when they are using unwholesome words. They have habitually communicated in this manner for so long they have become deaf to it. And when their spouse points it out, they respond with, "I'm sorry, I did not mean it," when the truth is, they did—How do we know?

> But the things that come out of the mouth come from the heart,
> and these things defile a man.[25]

Our words reveal what our heart contains. Anger, fear, or stress prevent us from filtering it. The words we speak reflect the attitudes of our hearts (good or bad).

1. In review of this list of unwholesome words, which ones do you believe are the greatest struggle for your spouse? _____
   _____
   _____

2. Which of these unwholesome words you guilty of? _____
   _____
   _____

Point:

Unwholesome words tear people down and destroy relationships. Sure, you may not always mean what you say, but your intentions cannot be swept under the rug. Our intent, sometimes, is to crush the other person's spirit.

21. Proverbs 13:18, 15:5, 16:2 (NASB)
22. Philippians 2:14 (NASB)
23. James 4:1–2 (NASB)
24. Proverbs 25:24 (NASB)
25. Matthew 15:18 (NASB)

Talking with Purpose:

You Must Only Communicate Words that Edify:

Let no unwholesome word proceed from your mouth, but only such a word as is *good* for *edification* according to the need of the moment, so that it will give grace to those who hear.[26]

Good:

Helpful, excellent, pleasant, good natured; gratifying, acceptable, valuable, precious, commendable—useful.

For Edification:

The act of building up, uplifting, enlightening, enhancing; for the betterment of someone or something. In Ephesians, edification refers to the act of promoting Christian growth in another, especially one's choice of words in the act of communicating with others.

Biblical ways that You can Edify Your Spouse:

- Listening and talking.[27]
- Avoiding tendencies to dominate the conversation.[28]
- Speaking the truth in love.[29]
- Allowing your spouse to express their thoughts and heart.[30]
- Expressing appreciation.[31]
- Through compliments and praise.[32]

26. Ephesians 4:29 (NASB)
27. James 1:19 (NASB)
28. Proverbs 10:19 (NASB)
29. Ephesians 4:15 (NASB)
30. 1 Peter 3:8 (NASB)
31. Romans 12:10 (NASB)
32. Philippians 4:14 (NASB)

- Giving your spouse the benefit of the doubt, without attempting to judge their motives.[33]
- Thinking before speaking.[34]
- Accepting constructive criticism.[35]
- Admitting your faults.[36]
- Considering all the facts before jumping to conclusions.[37]
- Taking responsibility when you are wrong.[38]
- Being willing to express forgiveness when offended.[39]
- Open, gentle correction, and humility.[40]
- Responding softly if your spouse is belligerent.[41]
- Allowing your spouse to speak without cutting them off.[42]
- Restating, in your own words, what you heard your spouse say to avoid misunderstandings.[43]
- Share your hurts and concerns without complaining, grumbling, or nagging.[44]
- Offering words of encouragement.[45]
- Phoning or writing.[46]
- Saying "I love you."[47]

---

33. Romans 14:13; 1 Corinthians 13:7 (NASB)
34. Proverbs 13:16 (NASB)
35. Proverbs 13:18 (NASB)
36. James 5:16 (NASB)
37. Proverbs 28:13 (NASB)
38. Proverbs 12:1 (NASB)
39. Luke 17:3–4 (NASB)
40. Galatians 6:1 3 (NASB)
41. Proverbs 15:1 (NASB)
42. Proverbs 18:1–2 (NASB)
43. Philippians 2:3–4 (NASB)
44. Galatians 6:2; Colossians 3:12–14 (NASB)
45. 1 Thessalonians 5:11 (NASB)
46. 3 John 1:13–14 (NASB)
47. John 13:34 (NASB)

- Asking for forgiveness.[48]
- Through self-sacrifice.[49]

1. Which items of the previous examples do you need to implement and do more of when you are communicating with your spouse? In other words, where do you need to improve? _____

   _____

   _____

2. Can you describe a time when your spouse used edifying words that had a positive effect on how you thought, felt, or acted? _____

   _____

   _____

3. In what ways are you communicating words that edify your husband or wife? _____

   _____

   _____

4. In what ways is your spouse a better person as a result of what you've said? _____

   _____

   _____

You Must Communicate Words Appropriate for the Moment:

> Let no unwholesome word proceed from your mouth, but only such a word as is good for edification according to the need of the moment, so that it will give grace to those who hear.[50]

Jeff and Nancy were on their way to a formal affair. Nancy had just finished dressing and putting on her jewelry when Jeff walked into the bedroom. "I know you're not wearing that dress," he said sharply. "What sale rack did you grab that from?" Nancy was surprised, offended, and felt insulted. With tear-filled eyes, she changed into another dress.

---

48. Ephesians 4:32 (NASB)
49. Romans 12:1–3, 14–21 (NASB)
50. Ephesians 4:29 (NASB)

The Result:

At the affair Nancy and Jeff barely spoke a word to each other. She now feels as if John is negatively judging what she wears and does not like how she looks even if he says nothing about it.

Couples can sometimes say things and give responses that are untimely and inappropriate. As a result, a spouse is offended, and the opportunity to edify and encourage them is lost by an inconsiderate reply and a sharp tongue. The heart can often blurt out hurtful words much easier and quicker than the mind can filter them. Many pleasant moments and experiences have turned sour because a spouse has said something that was discouraging at the wrong time in the wrong place.

1. Think of a time when your spouse blurted out a comment that was inappropriate. How did it make you feel and how did you respond? ___
   _____
   _____

2. On the other hand, describe a time when your spouse said something that was timely and according to the need of the moment: _____
   _____
   _____

Consider the wise words of King Solomon: "A man has joy in an apt (cheerful) answer, And how delightful is a timely word!"[51]

You Must Communicate Words That Give Grace to Everyone who Hears:

Let no unwholesome word proceed from your mouth, but only such a word as is good for edification according to the need of the moment, so that it will give grace to those who hear.[52]

51. Proverbs 15:23 (NASB)
52. Ephesians 4:29 (NASB)

Definition:

Grace:

Unmerited favor; merciful kindness; that which brings delight, joy, happiness, or good will.

Illustration:

Tyler decided to repair the water heater himself to save money against his wife, Megan's, wishes. After doing his research and purchasing all the supplies, he spent all day completing the job. The next day they arrived home from work to find the floors flooded and damaged from Tyler's substandard repairs. Megan was disappointed that Tyler chose to take on such a large job that was well-beyond his skill set. She resisted the temptation to say, "I told you so," and make Tyler feel guilty for the damaged floors they didn't have the money to repair. Megan chose to minister grace by encouraging Tyler. She comforted him by suggesting that had he not attempted the repair, the damage could have been much worse if the old, rusted unit had been ignored. She thanked him for his efforts. Megan decided to be an instrument of grace to her husband, who was already feeling defeated.

Scripture says, "Let your speech always be gracious, seasoned with salt, so that you may know how to answer everyone."[53] Our responsibility as Christians is to build up one another with our speech. A crushing word or response does just the opposite. Even if your spouse responds in an ungodly way, you can still take an opportunity to season your words with grace. In the similar way in which we use salt to make our food wholesome and palatable, Jesus said, "Salt is good, but if it loses its saltiness, with what will you season it? Have salt among yourselves and be at peace with one another."[54]

Before refrigeration, salt was used to preserve food and keep it from decaying. Once it had lost its preserving saltiness, it was thrown out. Scripture is encouraging us to have that preserving factor among one another to keep our relationships from decaying and going bad.

There will always be opportunities to show the grace of God in our hearts by communicating in a Christ-like manner. Giving grace, in some

---

53. Colossians 4:6 (NASB)
54. Mark 9:50 (NASB)

instances, may be achieved by what you do not say. For example, a wife can sanctify her husband without saying a word by her chaste and respectful behavior.[55]

> The truth is, When words are many, sin is unavoidable, but he who restrains his lips is wise.[56]

1. How do you respond to your spouse's failures and mistakes? _____
   _____
   _____

2. Has your spouse ever shared their problems with you, such as struggles at work or conflicts with family members or friends? If not, what do you believe is the reason? Do they generally feel better or worse after talking to you? Why or why not? _____
   _____
   _____

> He who restrains his words has knowledge, And he who has a cool spirit is a man of understanding. Even a fool, when he keeps silent, is considered wise[57]

The Effects of Words Spoken in the Right Circumstances:

> *Like* apples of gold in settings of silver is a word spoken in right circumstances. *Like* an earring of gold and an ornament of fine gold is a wise reprover to a *listening ear.*[58]

Avoid battering your spouse with words when they are already down. Although they may seem to have emotions made of steel, they need encouragement when they are discouraged or heavy with guilt. When they make mistakes, they are usually the one who feels the worst although they may not show it. Words of caution, reproof, or advice spoken wisely in love—at the right time, in the right circumstances—can be refreshing and

---

55. 1 Peter 3:1 (NASB)
56. Proverbs 10:19 (NASB)
57. Proverbs 17:27–28 (NASB)
58. Proverbs 25:11–12 (NASB; emphasis added)

beautifully-exquisite like fine silver and gold. Wise words bring hope and healing to a crushed, broken and grieving spirit.

Talking at Your Spouse versus Talking to Your Spouse:

John and Mary have been married for five years. They have three children, ages two, four, and five years old. John works, while Mary is a stay-at-home mom. The first four years of marriage was a financial strain on them. However, John recently received a promotion to an executive position and a tremendous increase in his annual salary. His income is now more than enough to meet their living expenses. However, John's promotion is demanding more hours. He now leaves for work at 7am and does not return until 8pm—Six days a week.

Mary is home to care for the children and perform domestic duties on her own. One evening, Mary reaches her breaking point. The two-year-old daughter throws her food and drink on the floor and begins to scream and cry for attention. While the four- and five-year-old are fighting over a toy, the younger child bites her sister on the arm. Cooking, cleaning, caring for the children, and doing laundry day in and day out has become more than Mary can bear. As soon as John arrives home and enters the front door, Mary has a few things to say.

Scenario One:

Mary yells, "John, I have had enough! I can't take it anymore. You are always gone so I am left here alone to deal with all these problems. Maybe you need to find another job because you are not the husband and father that you need to be. You are supposed to be the man of the house, but your job seems to come first before me and the children!"

Scenario Two:

She gently says, "John, I appreciate how hard you work. However, taking care of the kids and our home has been very stressful for me lately. The kids are sometimes out of control. I feel overwhelmed, and I feel all alone. The kids and I need you. We miss you. Can we schedule some quality time with the family as well as a date night with just the two of us? Besides, I could use a break. Let's come up with a plan."

1. In which scenario is Mary talking at John, and in which scenario is Mary talking to John? _____

   _____

   _____

2. What are your observations about the two scenarios? _____

   _____

   _____

   > There is one who speaks rashly like the thrusts of a sword, But the tongue of the wise brings healing.[59]

3. In Proverbs 12:18, what do you think it means to "speak rashly?" _____

   _____

   _____

4. In what ways is "speaking rashly" like the thrust of a sword? _____

   _____

   _____

5. Have you ever been cut, slashed, and stabbed by something your spouse said to you? If so, how did it affect you?

   Emotionally: _____

   _____

   _____

   Physically: _____

   _____

   _____

   Mentally: _____   _____

   _____

   _____

   Spiritually (your heart): _____

   _____

   _____

---

59. Proverbs 12:18 (NASB)

How did you respond? _____

_____

_____

6. Have you ever spoken rashly to your spouse? If so, how did it affect your relationship at that moment? _____

_____

_____

7. What are some of your words, rashly spoken, that you wish you could take back? _____

_____

_____

The Bible compares speaking rashly with being pierced with a sword. A sword is similar to, but longer than, an ordinary knife, and it is used for thrusting, slashing, or stabbing. It can be used to defend oneself or attack. Whether it is being used to protect or attack, being pierced by a sword can be fatal. The tongue is a small organ, but it can damage a relationship, often with life-long adverse effects. The Bible says the tongue gives life or death and can kill the spirit.

> How great a forest is set ablaze by such a small fire! And the tongue is a fire, a world of unrighteousness. The tongue is set among our members, staining the whole body, setting on fire the entire course of life, and set on fire by hell. For every kind of beast and bird, of reptile and sea creature, can be tamed and has been tamed by mankind, but no human being can tame the tongue. It is a restless evil, full of deadly poison. With it we bless our Lord and Father, and with it we curse people who are made in the likeness of God. From the same mouth come blessing and cursing. My brothers, these things ought not to be so.[60]

Imagine one small match from a book of paper matches. This little match can be used for good or evil. It can bring comfort or pain. It can be used to preserve life or destroy it. If this one tiny match is used carelessly, it can destroy the very structure you are in right now. So it is with the tongue. If you are reckless and careless with your words; it can cut, wound, maim, and hurt deeply. Often, words that are destructive and hurtful dwell in the hearts and minds of the offended for a lifetime. Conversely, a tongue used

60. James 3:3–10 (NASB)

wisely and with love can bring healing to the soul, encouragement, and hope to the spirit.

Talking at your spouse can be like the thrusts of a sword; it punctures and wounds the heart of the hearer, but talking to your spouse—with godly wisdom—brings healing to both the husband and wife, as well as to the relationship.

The tongue can be used as a deadly assault weapon. Scripture says words can bring life or death. Think about the damage your words can do. If you are guilty of assaulting your spouse with your tongue, ask for forgiveness no matter how long ago it has been. It is not better left in the past. The piercing of your words may have left a lasting wound, mark or scar. Your humble, loving words of contrition can bring healing and restoration to past and future years of emotional damage.

Common Examples of those who Talk *at* their Spouse Instead of *to* Them:

Talking *at* your spouse:	Talking *to* your spouse:	Scripture:
"Your problem is that you don't listen!"	"I would really like to express myself and for you to hear what I am saying."	2 Corinthians 6:11–13; Ephesians 4:15, 25; James 1:19
"I'm not talking about this right now!"	"This may not be the right time to talk about this. I'd like to discuss it after we've prayed about it and calmed down.	Proverbs 15:23, 17:14, 25:11–12
"Oh yeah, well what about you?"	"I'll take responsibility for that. I would like for you to take responsibility for your part."	Proverbs 12:1; Matthew 7:3–5; Romans 2:1, 3
"You Always . . . !" Or, "You Never . . . !"	"Sometimes you do this. I would like for you to try to do better in that area."	Deuteronomy 5:20; Proverbs 27:6a; 1 Thessalonians 5:14

73

Talking *at* your spouse:	Talking *to* your spouse:	Scripture:
"That's a lie. That's not what happened!"	"I would like you to understand what happened. Can I explain?	Proverbs 1:5; James 1:19
"You always take what I've said and spin it into an attack against you!"	"We can work this out if you could avoid reading any other meaning into what I've said."	Proverbs 18:1–2; Ephesians 4:25
"I'm done with this!"	"It does not look like we will resolve this now, but I want us to reconcile our differences in a loving way."	Romans 12:16–21, 14:19

The Difference Between "Talking at your Spouse" Versus "Talking to Your Spouse":

Listen to the words of Jesus:

> But I say to you that everyone who is angry with his brother shall be guilty before the court; and whoever says to his brother, "You good-for-nothing," shall be guilty before the supreme court; and whoever says, "You fool," shall be guilty *enough to go* into the fiery hell.[61]

In Matthew 5:22, there seems to be a correlation between anger and poor communication. The word "angry" in this text refers to the feelings and emotions you experience when you have been injured. It also relates to anger against a person without cause. Why is this anger without cause? It is because it is unjustified and rooted in sinful anger. It provokes an attack on the person and not the problem. Moreover, whoever relates to his neighbor (and your closest neighbor is your spouse) in this manner is said to be guilty.

But guilty of what? Of murder according to the previous verse.[62] Why? It is because it is rooted in sinful anger. It is all about the self. Also, it compels the injured person to point a finger, denounce, name-call, and hurl

61. Matthew 5:22 (NASB)
62. Matthew 5:21 (NASB)

74

insults towards the accused. Those who relate to others in this way will be held accountable by the one who is the supreme authority.

Sometimes husbands and wives talk at one another because they have been injured. Then, they express themselves and communicate with their mate out of anger. Pointing fingers, name calling, and hurling insults.

Proverbs 12:18 says, "There is one who speaks rashly like the thrusts of a sword." In contrast, Ephesians 4:15 states, "but speaking the truth in love, we are to grow up in all aspects into Him who is the head, even Christ."

Let's take a closer look at how it looks in practice as it relates to talking to your spouse versus talking at your spouse:

When you talk *at* your spouse:	When you talk *to* your spouse:
You express concern for yourself.	You express concern for your relationship.
You often place blame.	You share how you feel.
Your communication seems harsh, rude, or out of control and your spouse becomes defensive.	Your communication is loving, caring, and gentle, setting an environment for agreement and resolution.
You express that your spouse is the problem, and he or she needs to fix it.	You take responsibility for your contribution to the problem, admit your faults, ask for forgiveness, and work through the problem together.

The Main Issue:

Many couples communicate by verbally attacking their spouse. They fail to share how they feel, their struggles, hurts, and fears. Instead of pointing a finger at your spouse, chose words that expresses your heart, such as, "This is how I feel when this happens." Or, "This is how it makes me feel when you say this or do that."

Conclusion:

The purpose of this chapter is to help couples avoid the misery of destructive communication, to help, encourage, and equip married couples with the biblical tools they need to identify obstacles to effective communication so that they can establish biblical oneness as God has intended.

What are the Obstacles to Effective Communication?

1. Unwholesome words.
2. Failure to use words that edify.
3. Using words that are inappropriate for the need of the moment.
4. Uncontrolled tongue and using words to inflict pain on your spouse.
5. Refusing to show grace when offended.
6. Talking at your spouse in terms of finger-pointing, blame-shifting, and name-calling instead of talking to your spouse and sharing your heart.
7. Harboring anger towards your spouse.

We will discuss how to biblically overcome these obstacles to effective communication in the next chapter.

6

Communication

Part Two: Listening for Understanding

Purpose:

THE PURPOSE OF THIS chapter is to help, encourage, and equip married couples with biblical tools they need for effective communication so that their words and conversation build up, not tear down; to reflect the image of Christ and to establish biblical oneness as God has intended.

> Let all bitterness and wrath and anger and clamor and slander be put away from you, along with all malice. Be kind to one another, tender-hearted, forgiving each other, just as God in Christ also has forgiven you.[1]

Listening for Understanding:

It is more important to listen than it is to talk. You can not really know your spouse and become one with them if you are too busy talking instead of listening. Listening for understanding means you have trained your ears to hear the concerns, needs, hurt, or hope in your spouse's words and the expressions of their heart. Listening for understanding means you can filter out the details, discern the big picture, and hear what your spouse is communicating.

---

1. Ephesians 4:31–32 (NASB)

It is also important to hear what your spouse is communicating without words. Avoiding you, replying to you with short responses, and keeping busy to avoid engaging with you, may be some of the non-verbal communication you are getting. While these behaviors can become sinful, you must recognize that these behaviors may be evidence that your spouse want to be heard. You may or may not know what they are communicating, but you do know that they need you to listen for understanding.

> Let the wise hear and increase in learning, and the one who understands obtain guidance[2]

The Key to Effective Communication is Pursuing Christlikeness:

Believers are commanded to be open and honest and lovingly communicate words that edify the hearer. Excellent communication is not only about sharing your thoughts and concerns but a sincere attempt to understand the other person. However, communicating correctly according to God's standard does not come naturally, because at the core of most communication is the issue of the heart. Read the following verses and notice what the word of God says about tendencies of the heart and the relationship between how man communicates and his heart:

> The heart is more deceitful than all else And is desperately sick; Who can understand it?[3]

> He who separates himself seeks *his own* desire; He quarrels against all sound wisdom. A fool does not delight in understanding, But only in revealing his own mind.[4]

> You brood of vipers, how can you, being evil, speak what is good? For the mouth speaks out of that which fills the heart.[5]

> The good man out of the good treasure of his heart brings forth what is good; and the evil *man* out of the evil *treasure* brings forth what is evil; for his mouth speaks from that which fills his heart.[6]

2. Proverbs 5:1 (NASB)
3. Jeremiah 17:9 (NASB)
4. Proverbs 18:1–2 (NASB)
5. Matthew 12:34 (NASB)
6. Luke 6:45 (NASB)

Husbands and wives cannot exhibit good communication apart from Christ. The natural man is only concerned about being understood. Therefore, if you want to establish good communication with your spouse, you need the divine intervention of Christ and the Holy Spirit.

To talk at your spouse is like the thrust of a sword, but to talk to your spouse is to speak the truth in love, with tenderness!

How to Become an Effective Communicator:

Most devices that receive or send verbal communication have a volume button that is used to silence the communication. When couples display unloving attitudes and corrupt communication toward each other, they close the bridge of communication—one or both has turned off the volume and stopped listening.

Because of their spouse's history of corrupt communication, a husband or wife may assume that words will come with critical finger-pointing, ranting on and on, or lecturing. They have silenced communication and hindered any chance of verbally connecting with their spouse.

If your spouse has turned off the volume on you, he or she must begin to hear from you words of encouragement, support, self-control, and compassion that is needed to listen to your conversation and begin to value your words as necessary and comforting.

To keep the bridge of communication open between the two of you, you must consider the impact your words have on your spouse. If your spouse seems overly-sensitive and negatively-reactive to what you say, make sure you have not built up an insensitivity to your spouse's needs. It usually means your spouse needs encouragement from you. They also need encouragement from God's word about his or her worth, godly reproof, humility, and pride.

The Bridge of Communication:

There are unspoken actions and attitudes you must avoid in order to establish effective communication with your spouse.

Hatred and Bitterness:

Hatred is an emotion that stems from harboring unloving attitudes such as bitterness, resentment, unforgiveness, and ungodly anger. Sometimes an offended spouse will attempt to justify, ignore, or deny these attitudes. But the truth is they stir up strife (arguments and fights).

A person that feels hatred toward their spouse has written them off (murdered them) in their heart. Effective communication is always interrupted when a spouse injects feelings of unresolved bitterness, hatred and unforgiveness. These attitudes, according to the Bible, are sin issues that can never be justified, ignored, or denied.[7]

> Everyone who hates his brother is a murderer, and you know that no murderer has eternal life abiding in him.[8]

Jesus's sacrifice on the cross reconciled us to God and allowed for the forgiveness of our sins. This compels us to forgive others. If your spouse has sinned against you, communicate with your spouse in a way that encourages repentance. Effective, godly communication between you and your spouse should begin with confession, repentance, and forgiveness that restores your relationship.[9]

> and if he sins against you seven times in the day, and turns to you seven times, saying, "I repent," you must forgive him.[10]

> Brothers, if anyone is caught in any transgression, you who are spiritual should restore him in a spirit of gentleness. Keep watch on yourself, lest you too be tempted.[11]

> And we urge you, brothers, admonish the idle, encourage the fainthearted, help the weak, be patient with them all.[12]

---

7. Ephesians 4:31–32 (NASB)

8. 1 John 3:15 (NASB)

9. 1 Thessalonians 5:14 (NASB)

10. Luke 17:4 (NASB)

11. Galatians 6:1 (NASB)

12. 1 Thessalonians 5:14 (NASB)

Assumptions:

Assumptions can hinder marital communication and create conflict. Never assume you always know what your spouse is saying, thinking, or meaning. One spouse may assume they know what the other is about to say so they jump in to finish the statement and gear the conversation toward his or her assumption. A spouse can also assume they know what the other is thinking and begin a dialogue in response to those assumptions. A spouse may assume they know what their spouse means before they communicate what is on their mind. The spouse may even make false accusations based on those assumptions.

Regardless of how well you may think you know your spouse, don't assume you can speak for them or know every process of their thinking. Communicate with your spouse based on what he or she has expressed. Listen for understanding, and if you are not certain what they are expressing, then ask them to explain. A husband or wife who assumes they know their spouse so well they can speak or think for them has closed the bridge of communication and is more interested in proving what they think they know instead of making an effort to understand what their spouse is communicating.

> Spouting off before listening to the facts is both shameful and foolish.[13]

Avoidance:

Avoidance, shutting down and isolation, disconnects you from your spouse and makes it easy to harbor resentment. When communication with your spouse ends in arguments, criticism, or harsh words, it is easy to avoid talking or giving your opinion. Peace in your home sometimes means not communicating at all. But this is a false sense of peace. The more you shut down, the more distant you become. When couples fail to communicate in love there is separation and disunity.

> Rather, speaking the truth in love, we are to grow up in every way into him who is the head, into Christ, from whom the whole body, joined and held together by every joint with which it is equipped,

13. Proverbs 18:13 (NIV)

when each part is working properly, makes the body grow so that it builds itself up in love.[14]

Brooding:

Brooding (dwelling on unresolved issues, or wrong doings over an extended amount of time) will arouse wrath so problems must be dealt with before they get out of hand.[15]

> The beginning of strife is *like* letting out water, So abandon the quarrel before it breaks out.[16]

Example:

One purpose of a dam is to retain large amounts of water and restrict water flow in a specific area.

1. What could be the possible outcome if a dam has a small crack where water begins to seep through? _____

_____

_____

2. In considering Proverbs 17:14, how does the beginning of strife and the letting-out of water compare to a dam that has a crack? _____

_____

_____

3. When it comes to disagreements, what should you do to keep from making matters worse?[17] _____

_____

_____

If you want to establish effective communication between you and your spouse, there are certain actions and behaviors you must practice.

14. Ephesians 4:15–16 (NASB)

15. Proverbs 10:12, 17:14 (NASB)

16. Proverbs 17:14 (NASB)

17. Proverbs 17:14b (NASB)

Exhibit Self-control:

Have you ever had a cordial conversation with your spouse that spiraled into a heated argument? The reason conversations turn into severe arguments is due to the lack of self-control. Read the following verses and write down what each of them has to say about self-control. What do they say about your heart; your emotions; your thoughts; your words?

1. "Watch over your heart with all diligence, For from it *flow* the springs of life."[18] _____

   _____

   _____

2. "He who restrains his words has knowledge, And he who has a cool spirit is a man of understanding."[19] _____

   _____

   _____

3. "He who guards his mouth and his tongue, Guards his soul from troubles."[20] _____

   _____

   _____

4. "*Like* a city that is broken into *and* without walls Is a man who has no control over his spirit."[21] _____

   _____

   _____

5. "A time to tear apart and a time to sew together; A time to be silent and a time to speak."[22] _____

   _____

   _____

18. Proverbs 4:23 (NASB)
19. Proverbs 17:27 (NASB)
20. Proverbs 21:23 (NASB)
21. Proverbs 25:28 (NASB)
22. Ecclesiastes 3:7 (NASB)

6. "*We are* destroying speculations and every lofty thing raised up against the knowledge of God, and *we are* taking every thought captive to the obedience of Christ"[23] _____

_____

_____

7. "If anyone thinks himself to be religious, and yet does not bridle his tongue but deceives his own heart, this man's religion is worthless."[24]

_____

_____

Based on what you read thus far, how important is the control of your emotions, thoughts, and tongue as it relates to good communication? _____

_____

_____

If you want to establish effective communication between you and your spouse, there are certain actions and behaviors you must practice.

Practice Love that Revitalizes and Promotes Good Communication:

Counseling Issue:

Bob and Rachel have been married for five years and are having communication problems. Bob is an abstract communicator, while Rachel is concrete. Bob is a talker, and Rachel is generally a quiet person. Bob accuses Rachel of complete stonewalling. Stonewalling occurs when one spouse chooses to avoid or stop communicating. When she does speak, she gives concise short answers or says nothing at all.

The Result:

Bob and Rachel both complain that the other has a bad attitude. Bob is angry because Rachel does not talk to him. Rachel is frustrated and says Bob talks too much and that he is not a good listener.

---

23. 2 Corinthians 10:5 (NASB)
24. James 1:26 (NASB)

The Root of the Problem:

Most people who talk a lot are not good listeners. Rachel loves Bob, and she wants to communicate and share her heart with him. The problem is when she shares with Bob, he cuts her off when she is speaking. He is quick to analyze what she says, how she says it, and her choice of words. He claims he understands her problem and is always ready to provide a solution.

There is another issue with Bob that compels Rachel to stonewall: Whenever she makes attempts to share her struggles, whether it is issues on the job or with extended family, Bob is critical of her. He either finds fault or blames her for the issue. He has a habit of bringing up the past to point out what he believes she could do better. Rachel shuts down and stops communicating because she feels Bob is hyper-critical, insensitive, unsupportive, and not a good listener.

How can you practice Love that Revitalizes and Promotes Good Communication?

Do's and don'ts:	Biblical reference:
Be a good listener.	If one gives an answer before he hears, it is his folly and shame.[25]
Listen, not just with the ears, but with your heart. Try to understand and empathize with what your spouse is feeling.	Finally, all of you, have unity of mind, sympathy, brotherly love, a tender heart, and a humble mind[26]
Don't bring up old issues from the past, this implies unforgiveness and bitterness.	Forget the former things; do not dwell on the past[27]

25. Proverbs 18:13 (NASB)
26. 1 Peter 3:8 (NASB)
27. Isaiah 43:18 (NIV)

Do's and don'ts:	Biblical reference:
Do not keep a record of wrongs and use them as weapons.	Love is patient and kind. Love is not jealous or boastful or proud or rude. It does not demand its own way. It is not irritable, and it keeps no record of being wronged[28]
Identify and confront the problem. Do not attack the person.	Let no corrupting talk come out of your mouths, but only such as is good for building up, as fits the occasion, that it may give grace to those who hear.[29]
Be open and honest. Don't conceal your feelings or assume you spouse knows how you feel.	Rather, speaking the truth in love, we are to grow up in every way into him who is the head, into Christ.[30]
No matter what happens, reaffirm your love for one another, even if you disagree.	Hatred stirs up strife, but love covers all offenses.[31]

Replace your unloving attitudes with the love of Christ[32]

Let all bitterness and wrath and anger and clamor and slander be put away from you, along with all malice. Be kind to one another, tender-hearted, forgiving each other, just as God in Christ also has forgiven you.[33]

Seek to Overcome Evil with Good:

Chose to love unconditionally through humility, service, sacrifice, and giving, even when you believe your spouse does not deserve it. Love is a choice, not necessarily a feeling. To communicate effectively, you are going

28. 1 Corinthians 13:4–5 (NIV)
29. Ephesians 4:29 (NASB)
30. Ephesians 4:15 (NASB)
31. Proverbs 10:12 (NASB)
32. Ephesians 4:31–32 (NASB)
33. Ephesians 4:31–32 (NASB)

to have to let some things go. There are some unloving attitudes that you need to put off and replace those things with the love of Christ.

Put Off:

Things to stop doing.

Put On:

Things you should start doing.

If you are having trouble identifying what you need to put off, just ask your spouse. Often, the things you need to put off are the things your spouse complains about—that you may sometimes deny—as it relates to the way you communicate. Here are some examples of typical marital dialogues:

- "Why are you yelling?" "I'm not yelling!"
- "You sound angry." "I'm not angry."
- "I don't like your tone." "What tone?"
- "I'm looking at your face, and you look disgusted." "No, I'm fine."
- "That's not what I said." "I know, but what you are really trying to say is . . ."

Put-offs:	Put-ons:
Lying.	Speaking the truth in love.
Fleshly anger.	Godly anger.
Being concerned about getting.	Being concerned about giving.
Using words that tear down.	Using words that build up.
Bitterness: unloving attitudes.	Gladness of heart, kindness, tolerance, forbearance, goodness, controlling oneself when provoked.

Put-offs:	Put-ons:
Wrath and anger: internal or external violence; maybe kicking or throwing or breaking things, grinding teeth, biting bottom lip.	Tender-hearted, peaceful, quiet and calm, compassion, mercy.
Clamor and slander: outcry to others, ruining someone's reputation.	Forgiveness, grace, unmerited favor, pardoning of a penalty, not taking into account a wrong suffered, not reminding others of their misdeeds.
Malice: to plot evil against someone with the intent to cause harm.	Forgiving, being righteous towards others, and doing good to others regardless of feelings.

Summary of the Pathway to Good Communication:

Actions and attitudes that you must avoid in order to establish effective communication with your spouse:

- Hatred and bitterness.
- Assumptions.
- Avoidance.
- Brooding.
- Shutting down; stonewalling.
- Isolation.

If you want to establish Effective Communication between you and your spouse, there are certain actions and behaviors you must practice:

- Exhibit self-control.
- Practice real love that revitalizes and promotes good communication.
- Replace unloving attitudes with the love of Christ.[34]

34. Ephesians 4:31–32 (NASB)

You can become an effective communicator if you meditate on and apply Ephesians 4:29 to your life. It will affect every aspect of your life; it will impact your relationship with your spouse, children, family, friends, and most importantly, your fellowship with Christ.

What follows is an "Evidence of Bad Communication" worksheet. Circle the items you struggle with and also circle those that you believe your spouse may struggle with.

Evidence of Bad Communication Worksheet:

Instructions:

Read over the following lists and circle the items that are true of your inclinations in terms of how you communicate. Also circle those that you believe are relevant to the way your spouse communicates with you.

You:	Your spouse:
1. Talking too much and not listening.[35]	1. Talking too much and not listening.
2. Lying.[36]	2. Lying.
3. Cutting your spouse off while he or she is speaking.[37]	3. Cutting your spouse off while he or she is speaking.
4. Sarcasm.[38]	4. Sarcasm.
5. Facial Expressions that express extreme displeasure or anger (rolling of the eyes, smirks, squinting).[39]	5. Facial Expressions that express extreme displeasure or anger (rolling of the eyes, smirks, squinting).
6. Belittling.[40]	6. Belittling.

35. Proverbs 10:19; James 1:19 (NASB)
36. Ephesians 4:25 (NASB)
37. James 1:19 (NASB)
38. Ephesians 5:4 (NASB)
39. Genesis 4:5–6 (NASB)
40. Matthew 5:22 (NASB)

You:	Your spouse:
7. Exaggerating the facts or truth.[41]	7. Exaggerating the facts or truth.
8. Misreading meaning into something your spouse said.[42]	8. Misreading meaning into something your spouse said.
9. Becoming defensive when confronted with the truth.[43]	9. Becoming defensive when confronted with the truth.
10. Justifying your wrongs and refusing to take responsibility for your actions.[44]	10. Justifying your wrongs and refusing to take responsibility for your actions.
11. Drawing conclusions and giving an answer before hearing all the facts.[45]	11. Drawing conclusions and giving an answer before hearing all the facts.
12. Falsely accusing your spouse of something they have not done.[46]	12. Falsely accusing your spouse of something they have not done.
13. Making attempts to judge your spouse for what they do.[47]	13. Making attempts to judge your spouse for what they do.
14. Dominating conversations.[48]	14. Dominating conversations.
15. Being only concerned about your own opinion.[49]	15. Being only concerned about your own opinion.
16. Being quick-tempered.[50]	16. Being quick-tempered.

41. Numbers 13:32–33 (NASB)
42. Proverbs 15:4 (NASB)
43. James 5:16 (NASB)
44. Matthew 5:23–24 (NASB)
45. Proverbs 18:13 (NASB)
46. Exodus 20:16 (NASB)
47. James 4:11–12 (NASB)
48. Proverbs 10:19 (NASB)
49. Proverbs 18:1–2; Philippians 2:4 (NASB)
50. Proverbs 15:18, 29:11; Ephesians 4:26 (NASB)

You:	Your spouse:
17. Being too critical or fault-finding.[51]	17. Being too critical or fault-finding.
18. Cursing.[52]	18. Cursing.

After you have completed the "Evidence of Bad Communication" worksheet, schedule time to discuss your answers with your spouse.

First, discuss one item at a time and share what you circled for yourself and allow your spouse to do the same. Second, you and your spouse should take the opportunity to share items on the list that each of you circled in your assessment of one another.

If you circled an item for your spouse that your spouse disagrees with, you must give specific reasons why you circled that item along with real examples or incidents that support your perspective. If you can't think of a specific example to support your assessment, then the item must be struck from the list. The items that you and your spouse circled for one another should be a part of your list of put offs.

Now review the list of examples of words that edify from the previous chapter. Discuss which examples your spouse believes you should implement and how you can apply it in terms of how you communicate. This is your list of put-ons.

Discuss specifically what you are going to do to change—what you can do differently to apply it to your life as it relates to how you communicate. Ask your spouse what they believe you could do differently. Complete the "Plan for Improving Communication" worksheet on the next page.

Ground Rules:

Do not become defensive. Do not attempt to ignore, deny, or justify your bad communication. It should not be a "tit for tat" discussion centered around prideful attitudes. If anyone becomes angry or gets loud, the other person is to keep silent and simply stand to signify a violation of the ground

---

51. Proverbs 11:12–13, 25:9; Matthew 18:15 (NASB)
52. Proverbs 12:18, 15:1 (NASB)

rules. If the angry spouse does not settle down, end the discussion until another time, but it should resume sooner rather than later.

Plan for Improving Communication:

List of Put-offs: Items from the "Evidence of Bad Communication" worksheet that I need to stop doing.	List of Put-ons: Items from the "Words that Edify" list that I need to start doing.	Scriptures: Applicable Scripture relevant to this item of communication.	Plan for change: What am I going to do to apply this Scripture in how I communicate; what, specifically, am I going to do differently?

7

The Source of Conflict

When Your Pleasures Become Demands

Counseling Issue:

Tucker and Madison have been married for five years and have two children—until recently, both have had professional careers. Tucker was laid off from work four months ago, and he is having trouble finding a job. Since his unemployment, it seems they cannot have a decent conversation without it turning into a heated argument. They are experiencing more conversations that are erupting and escalating into full-blown conflicts.

In one incident, Tucker called a technician to their home to repair a broken garage door. Once the tech arrived, Tucker met with him, explaining the problem. The tech identified the problem, quoted a price, and Tucker consented on the spot. But before the tech could get started, Madison walked into the garage with a few questions of her own. Within a matter of minutes, Madison began to raise her voice at the tech, accusing him of price gouging and then asked him to leave. Here is a snapshot of Tucker and Madison's conversation in the garage for all the listening neighbors to hear:

Tucker: "You acted like a fool and disrespected me again."

Madison: "I did not disrespect you. I do not see how you could overpay for a repair without getting at least three estimates. It is not good business sense, and it is stupid. That is *not* how I do things."

Tucker: "Well, it is *your* fault that the garage door frame is broken in the first place, because of your constant carelessness of hitting it with your car."

Madison: "My carelessness? What about all the other things around the house that need repair that I have been bringing to your attention for months and still are not done? What kind of man neglects his own home?"

Tucker: "I told you would get to when I have time. You are nothing but a nagger. It is not like I do nothing around here. I cook, clean, and wash clothes."

Madison (with sarcasm): "Well, you have nothing else to do! You call yourself the man of the house, but you don't even have a job! A real man is supposed to provide for his family. I will respect you when you find a job!"

Tucker: "This conversation is over. I am done!"

At this point, Madison storms away and loudly slams the door. Tucker, steaming with anger, gets in his car and heads to the nearest bar. Over the next several days, Tucker sleeps on the sofa while Madison sleeps in a locked bedroom. They refuse to talk to one another even when asked a question. This is one of many incidents where their conversation has erupted to a mudslinging, brutal war. Tucker and Madison are experiencing extreme conflict.

What are your observations of the exchange between Tucker and Madison?

1. Expectations: _____
   _____
   _____

2. Differences: _____
   _____
   _____

3. Opinion of each other: _____
   _____
   _____

4. What do Tucker and Madison really want? _____
   _____
   _____

The Surface Problem:

Madison wants Tucker to find a job. Tucker wants Madison to stop nagging him.

The Real Problem:

Tucker wants to be respected. Madison wants Tucker to listen and value her input and opinion. Both desire something from the other and are displaying corrupt communication, sinful words and behavior because they are not getting what they want.

The Result:

Disunity, strife, anger, resentment, bitterness, hostility, poor communication, and disorder in the home.

Purpose:

The purpose of this chapter is to help couples understand the true source of conflict and help them avoid the misery of unresolved battles and discord.

What is Conflict?

Disagreements and quarrels are the most common terms used by couples to describe conflict. Since people have their own ideas as to what constitutes a conflict, let us differentiate between disagreements, quarrels, and conflict.

Disagreements:

Disagreements create occasions for conflict to occur. As we will see, disagreement and conflict are not the same. To disagree means to fail to agree, to have a difference of opinions, perspectives, or preferences. In a disagreement, people have ideas, views, and make choices that contradict one another. A disagreement occurs when a husband and wife see things from a different point of view.

Quarrels or Arguments:

The word quarrel means a heated verbal contention or argument. It is a stressed, strained, or severed relation that may persist beyond the contention.[1] It refers to an angry dispute or altercation, a spat or wrangle, or a disagreement marked by a temporary or permanent break in a friendly relationship. The biblical definition for quarrel is to engage in an argument with intense emotions. When a husband and wife are involved in a feud, they are going into verbal battle against one another.

Most often, when couples argue, they are verbally fighting over a specific issue. When exhausted, they may decide on a cease-fire because the discussion is not going anywhere. There may be a temporary shutdown of communication, and a momentary cease of physical intimacy. After things cool off, they settle down, conversation gradually resumes, and the relationship returns to something close to normalcy until the issue comes up again, which may send them into a quarreling tailspin once again.

Conflict:

The word conflict means a mental struggle resulting from incompatible or opposing needs, drives, wishes, or external or internal demands.[2] Conflict means to contest in warfare, to engage in combat—to collide or to clash. The Bible defines conflict as a war consisting of many battles. It means to clash severely, to struggle or fight. Conflict is not merely a battle, but it is a full-blown war that encompasses the whole range of hostilities. It involves enmity, bitterness, hatred, strife, resentment, belligerence, estrangement, aggression, retaliation, plotting, and scheming.

Couples experience conflict when simple disagreements become emotional, transitioning the dispute into a quarrel that is usually over a single issue. The argument then becomes a full-blown conflict when couples began bringing previous unrelated gripes, complaints, past offenses, or problems into the quarrel. They engage in a mudslinging contest, to the point where no one is listening to what the opposition is saying. The conflict escalates when someone says something that hits the other person below the belt. The injured recipient of the crushing blow may immediately respond with,

1. "Quarrel." Merriam Webster Dictionary.
2. "Conflict." Merriam Webster Dictionary.

"Oh, so you want to go there, huh?" The flames of the argument explode into an inferno.

Occasions for Conflict:

Personal preferences, differences of opinions, disagreements, and quarrels (arguments) are simply occasions for conflict and are not the source. Sometimes they can create an environment or conditions that are favourable for producing conflict. An example of the term "occasion" can be seen when meteorologists present weather forecasts. The weatherperson will often attempt to predict future weather based upon computer models that provide essential data and generate possible outcomes of weather conditions before it occurs. When hot and cold air meet rapidly, it creates an occasion for tornados. When warm ocean air rises, causing an area of lower air pressure below, that is an occasion for hurricanes to form. Excessive torrential rains over a long period is an occasion for massive flooding. Similarly, disagreements and arguments create occasions for conflict. Things that couples disagree on are endless. It is common for couples to disagree about:

- Communication methods: The best way to communicate. One spouse talks too much or not enough.

- Decision making: Should decisions be based on facts or facts plus feelings?

- Disciplining children: What is the best form of discipline for our children; should we spank or not; should we have long talks or administer punishment?

- Driving directions: What is the best way to get to where we are going? If we are lost, should we stop and ask someone for directions or keep driving?

- Friends: Are opposite-sex friends permissible in our marriage? How much time or influence should be allowed from single friends? Are there any relationships we need to sever?

- Getting things done: Is my way the best, or is your way best? Whose idea are we going to use?

- Intimacy: What constitutes quality time together; staying home, or going out? Should I always buy flowers and chocolates, or are romantic words in a card enough?

- Making purchases: Should we buy a new home or rent; should we purchase a car or lease?

- Managing money: Should we spend or save? Are you spending too much; are you a tightwad? Which one of us is the best person to manage our finances?

- Traditions: Should we hold to my family traditions or yours; should we make our own family traditions?

- Morals: Whose views of what is morally right and wrong are correct?

- Past: Should we hold onto the past or let it go?

- Political views: Capitalism or socialism; liberal or conservative?

- Priorities: What may be a priority for you is not a priority for your spouse.

- Relationships with in-laws: How much time should we spend with in-laws? What is the best way to resolve strained relationships with in-laws or extended family members; should we reach out to them or avoid them?

- Religious perspectives: views about God, the Bible, Christ, and Scripture interpretation.

- Repairs: Do we need to go with the first quote from a reliable company, or should we get multiple quotes? What is a reasonable price?

- Sex: Once a day, once a week, or once a month?

- Shopping styles: Do we take our time in stores or do we get in and get out?

- Time management: What is the best way to manage our time? Should it be time with kids, with one another, or some "me time?" What should I do with my spare time?

Anything you keep outside of the marriage union will induce conflict. Money, friendships, loyalties to other people, time, affections, secrets kept, or things you perceive to be out of your spouse's jurisdiction will induce conflict. These are things you have not fully vested in the marriage relationship—you have placed them outside of your marriage union and they are also outside of God's will for your marriage.

Things that couples disagree on are endless. However, conflict is not the same as a disagreement. A disagreement involves differences of opinion and personal preferences. Opposing viewpoints do not equate to conflict. Your disputes are simply occasions for battle and not the source. Moreover, personality and historical differences can also create occasions for conflict. Who you are as a person in comparison to your spouse is never the source of conflict. Sadly, couples will attempt to use "irreconcilable differences" as a justifiable reason for getting a divorce, but the truth is, irreconcilable differences are an occasion for conflict, leading to divorce. The fact is you and your spouse both have historical differences and experiences that have helped shape your character. You and your spouse are naturally different. Here are some common areas where you and your spouse may be experiencing differences:

- Admitting wrongs: Do you often admit your faults and ask for forgiveness, or rarely admit mistakes and ask for forgiveness although you are aware of the wrongs committed?

- Decision-making: Are you a quick decision-maker without much thought, or do you take your time and consider all the facts and "what ifs?"

- Education: GED, high school diploma, undergraduate degree, Bachelor's, or Doctorate?

- Expressing emotions: Are you externalizing and quick to say how you feel, or internalizing and reluctant to say how you feel about something?

- Handling finances: Saver, spender, greedy, or charitable?

- Historical background: How were you raised? What is your socioeconomic status; what about previous relationships or family relationships?

- Parenting skills: Are you a disciplinarian or permissive and lenient?

- Personalities: Fast or slow, driven or laid back, domineering or passive, talkative or quiet?

- Planning: Do you believe that planning is essential and do not like surprises, or do you enjoy spontaneity, going with the flow, and love surprises?

- Resolving problems: Let's fix it and deal with it, right here right now, or wait until after you take time to process the information?

- Sexual needs: How often?

- Showing affection: Do you like to cuddle and be touched, or are you not the affectionate type?

- Socializing: Extrovert or introvert?

- Religion: Religious experiences and practices.

- Timeliness: Do you Need to be on-time and hate to be late, or are you often late because being on time is no big deal?

- Togetherness: Do you need quality time together or need some "me" time?

As you consider this list, you can see that you and your spouse are different. You both may be alike in some ways, but chances are your differences outnumber your similarities. Most of the differences you exhibit are neutral, that is, the Bible does not label it as a sin issue. On the other hand, some of the character traits you and your spouse exhibit are blatant sins. We will shed more light on this subject ahead. The fact remains that we are all different, and we have different opinions and view things differently. Your differences are never the source of conflict but are merely occasions for conflict.

Where Does Conflict Come From?

Ungodly conflict is rooted in worldliness.

> Who among you is wise and understanding? Let him show by his good behavior his deeds in the gentleness of wisdom. But if you have bitter jealousy and selfish ambition in your heart, do not be arrogant and *so* lie against the truth. This wisdom is not that which comes down from above, but is earthly, natural, demonic. For where jealousy and selfish ambition exist, there is disorder and every evil thing.[3]

1. James asks, "who among you is wise and understanding?"

Define "wise": _____
_____
_____

---

3. James 3:13–16 (NASB)

Define "understanding": _____

_____

_____

2. Read the following verses and write down what they say about wisdom, knowledge, and understanding:

Psalms 111:10: _____

_____

_____

Proverbs 1:7: _____

_____

_____

Proverbs 2:6: _____

_____

_____

Proverbs 11:12, 14:29: _____

_____

_____

Job 28:20, 28: _____

_____

_____

Matthew 7:24: _____

_____

_____

James 1:5: _____

_____

_____

3. What is the evidence that you are both wise and understanding as in James 3:13? _____

_____

_____

4. The word "gentleness" in James 3:13 means humility. In what ways are "humility" and "wisdom" related and why are they? _____

_____

_____

In James 3:13, the author presents evidence of someone truly wise and understanding. Then he gives contrast to godly wisdom and understanding. He says, "But if you have bitter jealousy and selfish ambition in your heart, do not be arrogant and *so* lie against the truth. This wisdom is not that which comes down from above, but is earthly, natural, demonic. For where jealousy and selfish ambition exist, there is disorder and every evil thing."[4]

5. The word for bitter jealousy is where we get our English word "envy." Define the word "envy": _____

_____

_____

In James 3:14–16, selfish ambition is the Greek word, *eritheia*, which means ambition, self-seeking, rivalry, and party-making.[5] In essence, the word can be used to describe the ambition of those who are self-seeking opportunists.

6. How would you describe "selfish ambition?" _____

_____

_____

7. Where does "envy" and "selfish ambition" reside? According to James, where is their place of origin, and is it always detectible? _____

_____

_____

8. Some political leaders lash out when people accuse them of wrong doing or when their character is under attack. With this in mind, what does envy, and selfish ambition have to do with arrogance and lying?

_____

_____

4. James 3:14–16 (NASB)

5. Vine, *Vine's Expository Dictionary*, Strong's Greek 2052.

"This wisdom is not that which comes down from above, but is earthly, natural, demonic."[6]

9. Where do envy, selfish ambition, arrogance, and lying come from? __
   _____
   _____

James says that the evidence of this kind of wisdom is disorder and every evil thing.

10. What is "disorder" and what does disorder look like in a marriage? __
    _____
    _____

11. What does evil look like in marriage? In other words, what are some of the evil things spouses do to one another when they are angry or don't get what they want? _____
    _____
    _____

Application:

If you have envy and selfish ambition in your heart, you are operating in the ways of the world (earthly), the sinful nature of the flesh (natural), and under demonic influences. It starts with envy, which is to fervently want what another has and to be angry with them because they have it, and you don't. Your spouse has something in their control to give that you are burning for. You lust after what he or she has. What you want becomes a demand. They refuse to give you what you want, or they give you something that you don't want. So, you become angry.

You want what you want because of selfish ambition. The very thing that you demand is for your own benefit (such as affection), not your spouse's. When your spouse discerns your real motive, you may display arrogance and lie to conceal your agenda.

Your response to being accused might be "How dare you to accuse me of that! How can you say such a thing about me? I am just looking out for what is best for our relationship." This is arrogance and a lie.

---

6. James 3:15 (NASB)

But the wisdom from above is first pure, then peaceable, gentle, reasonable, full of mercy and good fruits, unwavering, without hypocrisy. And the seed whose fruit is righteousness is sown in peace by those who make peace.[7]

Apostle James paints a vivid picture of how godly wisdom and understanding compare to worldliness. Then he furthers the idea by giving a picture of what worldliness looks like in our life.[8] We will elaborate more on the correlation between godly wisdom and understanding and resolving conflict in the next chapter. Before we continue our discussion regarding the source of conflict, let's take a moment to identify some of your desires.

Identifying your Pleasures:

What are some things you expect from your husband or wife? What are things that you want from your spouse that he or she has in their power to give? What are some of your desires? Next, put a circle around each unmet expectation.

Expectations of my wife:	Expectations of my husband:

7. James 3:17–18 (NASB)
8. James 4:1–3,11–12 (NASB)

What is the Source of Conflict?

> What is the source of quarrels and conflicts among you? Is not the source your pleasures that wage war in your members? You lust and do not have; *so* you commit murder. You are envious and cannot obtain; *so* you fight and quarrel. You do not have because you do not ask. You ask and do not receive, because you ask with wrong motives, so that you may spend *it* on your pleasures.[9]

Using a dictionary and scriptures provided, define the following terms and answer the final question:

1. Source: _____

   _____

2. Pleasures (Titus 3:3): _____

   _____

3. Wage (Romans 6:13, 19, 7:23): _____

   _____

4. War: _____

   _____

5. Lust: _____

   _____

6. Murder: _____

   _____

7. Envious: __ _____

   _____

8. Motives: _____

   _____

9. James 4:1–3 (NASB)

9. In one sentence, please summarize the meaning of James 4:1–3: _____

_____

_____

Desires that Become Commands Breed Conflict:

In James 4:1, the writer of this epistle poses a question. He asks, "What is the source of quarrels and conflicts among you?" Then James pointedly answers his initial question with another question, a statement of fact; he says, "Is not the source Your Pleasures that wage war in your members?" What pleasures is Apostle James referring to? The word "Pleasure" can be defined as the state or feeling of being pleased.[10] As a verb, the word refers to that which brings delight or gratification. However, the Greek word for pleasure that James uses in this verse carries a much stronger meaning than the English definition. The term pleasure in this text means to have a burning desire and passion for something pleasurable. It is to have a desire, appetite, or to lust.[11]

To wage war means to plot, plan, and develop a strategy to defeat an opposing force. A commander of an army must be knowledgeable of his opponent if he wants to be victorious. To win a war, a commander must consider and identify the weaknesses of the opponent.

But where does the waging of war take place? James says, "your pleasures that wage war" are "in your members!" It takes place on the inside of us, in our heart, evidenced by how we relate to the person we are in conflict with.

Consider the expectations and pleasures that you listed on the "Identifying Your Pleasures" worksheet. What would you say is the source of quarrels and conflict among you, and what is it that compels you to wage war against one another? Is it not your pleasures and expectations—things that you desire, need, lust for, want—that wage war on the inside? The very things that you take pleasure in or need and want are not for your spouse's benefit but your own.

James says you burn for things, and when you do not receive what you want, you commit murder. But you may object with, "But I am not

10. Merriam Webster Dictionary

11. Zodhiates, *The Complete Word Study Dictionary: New Testament*, Strong's Greek 2237.

a murderer!" The truth is, all of us commit murder when we engage in full-blown conflict. How do we murder our spouse? We murder with our hearts, in terms of our attitudes such as bitterness, resentment, hatred, anger, displeasure, wrath, and sinful anger. When we regard a person as a "no good so and so" in our hearts, then we are guilty of murder! We murder our spouse when we are denouncing them as a person and view them as a deplorable or worthless individual. We murder them with our words. We commit murder when we audibly point out their weaknesses, past failures, character flaws, inadequacies, their struggles and shortcomings, habits, hang-ups, and their faults. We bring up past offenses and use them as weapons and ammunition to hurt them.

We also murder with our behavior when we refuse to communicate through shutting down, avoidance, isolation, neglecting spousal responsibility, and withholding physical intimacy. We attack or reject our spouse by malicious behavior and being passive-aggressive. Behavior such as not cooking, not cleaning, staying late at work to keep from going home, not answering the phone or returning phone calls, or sending provocative long text messages in large caps. We murder them by sharing shameful or embarrassing information about them with others or on social media to destroy their reputation. We may purposely neglect our marital responsibilities in an attempt to retaliate until we get what we want.

In Conflict, Your Demands Become Law:

> Do not speak against one another, brethren. He who speaks against a brother or judges his brother, speaks against the law and judges the law; but if you judge the law, you are not a doer of the law but a judge *of it.* There is *only* one Lawgiver and Judge, the One who is able to save and to destroy; but who are you who judge your neighbor?[12]

How is James 4:11–12 related to James 4:1 3? In James 4:1–3, the writer says that the source of quarrels and conflict is our desires that become demands. When our spouse fails to meet our expectations, we tend to speak against them. We may be reluctant to say what we want to say to their face because it would be highly offensive. Although in our hearts we condemn them because they have refused to give us what we want. In James 4:11–12, our demands have become law. We place ourselves as a judge of the law. We

12. James 4:11–12 (NASB)

hold a court hearing and put them on trial. In the court we are the judge, jury, the prosecuting attorney, and the bailiff. We accuse them of breaking our law, and we declare them guilty as charged. Then, we sentence our spouse with a penalty and punishment for breaking our law.

Our punishment may be avoidance, refusing to talk to them, withholding sex, refusing to help in the household, or withholding affection or compassion. Then after two days, or two weeks, or thirty days of punishment, we might consider granting them probation. But are we qualified to judge? Yes, we are qualified to judge wrong behavior.[13] Let's take a look at examples of wrong behavior by completing the quiz that follows.

Quiz:

How has your spouse wronged you? How has he or she sinned against you? Place a "Y" for yes and "N" for no to the following statements:

Has Your Spouse Ever:

_____ Lied to you

_____ Disrespected you

_____ Refused to communicate

_____ Failed to do what they said they would do, when they said they would do it

_____ Refused to listen when you are talking

_____ Refused to embrace your opinion

_____ Wrongly accused you

_____ Became angry with you

_____ Refused to admit faults or ask for forgiveness when they knew they were wrong

_____Criticized you

_____ Became defensive when approached about a specific issue

_____ Used harsh words when speaking to you

13. James 5:19–20; John 7:24; Matthew 18:15–17 (NASB)

_____ Was insensitive to your feelings

_____ Maximized your wrongs while minimizing his or her own

_____ Complained and grumbled

_____ Exhibited a bad attitude

_____ Said something inappropriate for the moment

_____ Made you feel unloved

How many of the previous examples of wrong behavior did you write "Y" for your spouse?

_____

Since you have been married or engaged, how many of the examples of wrong behavior are you guilty of yourself? Have *you* ever lied to your spouse? Do you ever grumble or complain? Have you ever refused to communicate? Are you a good listener? Do you become defensive when approached about a matter? If you answer "yes" for yourself to any of the items listed, then you are disqualified to judge! A lawbreaker is prohibited from judging another lawbreaker when he is guilty of the same offense.

James says, "There is *only* one Lawgiver and Judge, the One who is able to save and to destroy; *but who are you who judge your neighbor?*"[14]

> For with the judgment you pronounce you will be judged, and with the measure you use it will be measured to you.[15]

We are called to Judge wrong doing but never to condemn! The truth is when we pronounce judgment upon others, we are also condemning ourselves. Why? Because we are usually guilty of doing the same thing. God is the only true and righteous judge—not you.

Our motive in conflict is to get what we want from our spouse and to make them pay the penalty for not meeting our demand. Then we dare to take the matter to God in prayer, but God refuses to answer. Why? James says, "You do not have because you do not ask. You ask and do not receive, because you ask with wrong motives, so that you may spend *it* on your pleasures."[16]

14. James 4:12 (NASB)

15. Matthew 7:2 (NASB)

16. James 4:3 (NASB)

Why are your motives wrong? Some of the things you want, desire, or need from your spouse are reasonable. Some things you take pleasure in may also be neutral. They are not necessarily sinful. But your motives become wrong when the reason for your pleasures are all about you without consideration for anyone or anything else. Your motives may be disguised as something for the benefit of others, but it is what *you* desire for them. You can recognize it is a wrong motive and sinful when you exhibit an ungodly response when you do not get what you want.

Conclusion:

Your pleasures quickly become sinful when your neutral desires, needs, or wants began to burn within you. You lust for it to the point where it becomes a demand, when it becomes something that you must have and refuse to take no for an answer. At that point, the things you want is not about pleasing God, or for the benefit of your spouse, your children or anyone else. It is about *your* desires, needs, and wants. It is all about what makes *you* happy or content. It is about what satisfies *you*. During a conflict, your motives for wanting what you want become deeply embedded in self-gratification. Why? Because our intent is not to glorify God but to glorify self and the fulfillment of our pleasures.

1. What can you do to avoid conflict?
2. What do you do when you find yourself in conflict?
3. How do you go about reconciling and restoring a loving relationship with your spouse after conflict?

We will provide answers to these and other questions in the next chapter.

8

The Solution to Conflict

Putting God and Your Spouse Before Your Pleasures

Counseling Issue:

KEN AND LISA HAVE been married for three years and have a four-year-old son. Lisa wants their son to attend a highly-competitive private school that ranks among the top in the state. Ken is less concerned about their son's college prep right now. Ken prefers that he attend a neighborhood school whose district ranks high in standardized test, where he can attend with the kids in his community.

Lisa is adamant about enrolling their son in this school and is afraid they may lose the opportunity to get him in due to the enrollment wait list. Ken is considering all the specifics: their son's temperament, transportation, after-school activities, plus the fact that the tuition is not something they planned for in their budget.

Ken accuses Lisa of being more concerned about having their child in this private school and less concerned about his emotional and social development. Lisa accuses Ken of being too limited in his thinking. She says he is not concerned enough about their son's future and putting him ahead of the curve. She wants Ken to understand her point of view and agree that her choice is the best. Ken wants Lisa to see that he is right; he believes Lisa should forget about it and submit to his decision.

The Result:

This couple is experiencing major conflict. Lisa is angry because Ken does not agree with her decision. She does not communicate with Ken and when he asks her a question she says, "whatever, it doesn't matter." Ken has taken a resolute approach and refuses to discuss it any longer. He is angry because Lisa will not submit. In response, he spends as much time away from home as possible.

The Problem (The Source of their Conflict):

Lisa wants Ken to agree with her philosophy about their son's education. Ken wants Lisa to submit to him, even if she does not agree. Conflict occurs when desires, wants, and needs become demands.

Purpose:

The purpose in this chapter is to help couples avoid the misery of constant conflict; to give married couples the necessary tools they need to respond to conflict with love and in a spirit of Christ-like humility; to maintain marital unity that's saturated in unconditional love and brings glory and honor to God.

As stated in the previous chapter, the sinful desires of our flesh are the source of conflict. It stems from an unbiblical response to not getting what we want, or when we are getting behaviors and actions from others we do not want. Some of the things you desire are reasonable, neutral, and are not necessarily sinful. However, your pleasures quickly become sinful when neutral desires, needs, or wants begin to burn within you to the point where they become a demands. When your spouse has the ability or power to give it and refuses, your sinful response is the root cause of the conflict. At that point, the things you want is all about your desires, needs, and wants. It is all about what makes you happy and content. It is about what satisfies you. During a conflict, your motives for wanting what you want becomes deeply embedded in self-gratification. Why? Because your intent is not necessarily about glorifying God, but it is about glorifying self in pursuit of personal fulfillment of your pleasures.

As believers, your goal in life is to be pleasing to God. The Apostle Paul wrote, "So, we make it our goal to please him, whether we are at home in the body or away from it."[1]

Now that we have briefly reviewed the source of conflict, from a biblical perspective, let us discuss the biblical solution to conflict.

The Biblical Solution to Conflict:

Do nothing from selfishness or empty conceit, but with humility of mind regard one another as more important than yourselves; do not *merely* look out for your own personal interests, but also for the interests of others.[2]

Brethren, even if anyone is caught in any trespass, you who are spiritual, restore such a one in a spirit of gentleness; *each one* looking to yourself, so that you too will not be tempted.[3]

Do nothing from selfishness and for personal gratification.[4]

The apostle Paul says in Philippians 2:3 that we should do nothing from selfishness and empty conceit. The original text reads, "nothing according to contention, or vainglory." It says that we are to do nothing—not one thing—that comes down from, aligns with, or stems from contention. The word contention refers to any acts that are driven by self-interest, selfish ambition, or personal gain. The writer warns that we should avoid doing anything from selfish motives that cause fights, creates battles, and friction.

Paul also says we must avoid doing anything for vainglory. The word vain carries the idea of a person who is prideful, arrogant, boastful, and having an inflated view of one's importance, gifts, abilities, and intellect. A vain person embraces the illusion that he is superior to another. The term "glory" in Philippians 2:3 means to seek the praise, acknowledgment, recognition, or honor of others—even by being pretentious. In essence, "vainglory" means to have an inflated view of oneself and to seek the praise and recognition of another. A person who exhibits contention (selfishness) and

1. 2 Corinthians 5:9 (NIV)
2. Philippians 2:3–4 (NASB)
3. Galatians 6:1 (NASB)
4. Philippians 2:3a (NASB)

vainglory will often pursue self-gratification at the expense of causing strife and friction with others, even if it means severing relationships.

So how do contention and vainglory apply to you? If you want to avoid ungodly conflicts with your spouse, the first thing you must do is realize that your marital relationship is not all about you. Your marriage does not revolve around your happiness. Your spouse is not there to satisfy your every desire, expectation, and demand. The role of your spouse is not to fulfill your pleasures. Your spouse is not merely there to meet all of your needs. It is not about getting everything you want to elevate yourself or prove that you are right, and they are wrong. It is not about who wins the battle. It is not a competitive sport, where the winner takes home the prize. Marriage is not an avenue for self-glorification nor praise and recognition. Marriage is about loving your spouse unconditionally. Unconditional love requires self-denial, sacrifice, and giving, not because they deserve it, but because it brings glory to God. Jesus said the following words: "But love your enemies, and do good, and lend, expecting nothing in return; and your reward will be great, and you will be sons of the Most High; for He Himself is kind to ungrateful and evil *men*." In conflict, your spouse can sometimes appear as though he or she is your enemy.[5]

Review Point 1:

If you are going to avoid unnecessary conflict, you must do nothing from selfishness or empty conceit—you must exhibit humility.

> Do nothing from selfishness or empty conceit *but with humility of mind* regard one another as more important than yourselves[6]

The Humility of Mind:

This term means to have lowliness of mind, to view oneself from God's perspective, and to think of oneself as insignificant in comparison to the greatness of God. When you see yourself in light of the awesomeness, the splendor, and majesty of God, it compels a spirit of humility. A distorted view of God leads to an inflated opinion of self. When you embrace the

5. Luke 6:35 (NASB)
6. Philippians 2:3b (NASB)

fact that you are a sinner saved by grace, it causes humility to infiltrate an otherwise prideful heart. Humility is the lowliness of spirit and mind: "For a sinner, Humility involves the confession of his sin and a deep realization of his unworthiness to receive God's marvelous grace."[7]

What does Humility Look Like in Practice?

Read the following verse:

> Therefore I, the prisoner of the Lord, implore you to walk in a manner worthy of the calling with which you have been called, with all humility and gentleness, with patience, showing tolerance for one another in love, being diligent to preserve the unity of the Spirit in the bond of peace.[8]

Attributes of Humility:

- Gentleness: Mildness of attitude and behavior; meekness; respectable; void of hostility and aggression; enduring with patience when injured by others.

- Patience: Showing self-restraint even when provoked or annoyed, without complaining or becoming irritated.

- Showing tolerance in love: To put up with another; to tolerate in love without having an attitude; to bear up and endure the imperfections and faults of another.

- Persevering unity: To work hard to establish and maintain oneness in relations with another; striving for togetherness; to protect from disunity.

- Peace: Harmonious relationships that are free from worry; to have tranquility, to make a truce.

Notice that the characteristics of humility are also expressions of the fruit of the spirit.

---

7. Zodhiates, *The Complete Word Study Dictionary: New Testament*, Strong's Greek 5012.

8. Ephesians 4:1–3 (NASB)

But the fruit of the Spirit is love, joy, peace, patience, kindness, goodness, faithfulness, gentleness, self-control; against such things, there is no law.[9]

Attributes of humility are the attributes of Christlikeness.

Have this attitude in yourselves which was also in Christ Jesus, who, although He existed in the form of God, did not regard equality with God a thing to be grasped, but emptied Himself, taking the form of a bond-servant, *and* being made in the likeness of men. Being found in appearance as a man, He humbled Himself by becoming obedient to the point of death, even death on a cross.[10]

Review Point 2:

If you want to avoid conflict, you must exercise humility! You must view your spouse as more important than yourself.

Do nothing from selfishness or empty conceit but with humility of mind *regard one another as more important than yourselves*[11]

In Philippians 2:3, the Apostle Paul wrote that we ought to regard one another as more important than ourselves. The word "regard" here means to hold a particular mindset, to believe, or to embrace a positive view about another person. The phrase, "as more than important," means to hold above or to value one thing over another. In essence, the term means to consider another person as more valuable than yourself.

Paul is not suggesting that you view others as better than yourself, he is merely saying that you should see others as worthy of more consideration than you already give yourself. What is interesting is, this phrase is just the opposite of relating to others from "selfishness and empty conceit." Moreover, the phrase, "*regard one another as more important than yourselves*" is often practiced among couples who are in the dating stage of their relationship.

Usually, when couples are dating, each person makes deliberate attempts to present their best to the other person—back rubs are voluntary.

9. Galatians 5:22–23 (NASB)

10. Philippians 2:5–8 (NASB)

11. Philippians 2:3 (NASB)

Whatever restaurant you want to go to is always fine. What to do on date night is at the discretion of the other person. During the dating stage, couples lovingly and patiently compete in showing how they can please the other, regarding the other as more important than themselves. Here is an example of a typical dialogue between a dating couple:

"What do you want for dinner?"

"Oh, I don't know—whatever you want."

"It doesn't matter to me!"

"What about Chinese food?"

"That sounds good to me!" (Even though he hates Chinese food).

These types of dialogues continue in just about every subject matter in the relationship. What is happening here? Each person regards the other person as more than themselves.

Each of them views one another worthy of more consideration than themselves. But isn't it strange how quickly things change after couples say, "I do?" Conflict begins to erupt more often in the relationship. Why do things change? Each person is expecting the same consideration from the other that they were receiving when they were dating. When they were dating, they both were giving more than they were taking. The problem is they both remain takers, but they are no longer givers. The idea is, "If you don't give to me, then I am not giving to you." Now they begin to experience conflict in their marriage. Why? Because their relationship has shifted to one where both parties are operating according to selfishness, in the pursuit of personal benefits: Selfishness and empty conceit.

How Important Are You?

Everyone has value. Everyone has gifts, talents, and abilities. Your spiritual gifts are unique gifts that you possess to be used in serving others in the kingdom of God. The gift of teaching, exhortation, compassion, and giving are just a few attributes of spiritual gifts.

1. What are some of your gifts? _____
   _____
   _____

2. How are your gifts important? _____
   _____
   _____

Talents are natural, God-given abilities that you possess since birth. Some people are born with the physical ability to run fast, the cognitive ability to retain vast amounts of information, or with the ability to sing with a beautiful voice.

1. What are some of your talents? _____
   _____
   _____

2. How are your talents important? _____
   _____
   _____

Your abilities are things that you have learned to do in life over the years through experience, practice, trial, and error. For example, some people can cook delicious meals, many of them are chefs. Some people who are good with numbers and accounting are CPAs. Many people who developed the ability to strike a golf ball well are on the PGA tour.

1. What are some of your abilities? _____
   _____
   _____

2. How are your abilities important? _____
   _____
   _____

Sometimes, we determine our self-worth based upon our gifts, talents, and abilities—they are vital to us. You have ideas and opinions about life, you may even have short-term or long-term goals. You have views on moral issues. You have wants, needs, and things that you desire. Are these things an essential part of who you are? Sure they are! But the real question is, do you view your spouse as more important than how you already see yourself?

If the answer is no, then you may be viewing yourself from the wrong vantage point. If your view of yourself is based solely upon your abilities, gifts, talents, and reasoning, then you will—more than likely—relate to your spouse with selfishness and empty conceit. Man's natural tendency is to have an inflated view of himself based on his accomplishments and abilities. As such, man tends to think more highly of himself than he is. The Bible warns against this.

> For through the grace given to me I say to every man among you not to think more highly of himself than he ought to think; but to think so as to have sound judgment, as God has allotted to each a measure of faith.[12]

The only way you can view your spouse as more significant than yourself is through humility. Humility is only obtainable when you are able and willing to see yourself from God's perspective. When you recognize just how great God is and how insignificant you are—and the fact that God loves you enough to send his son to pay the penalty for your sin so that your sins are forgiven not based on merit, gifts, abilities, and talents but grace—then it should stimulate a heart of humility, thanksgiving, and worship. A godward mindset compels you to view your spouse as more important than yourself.

> What is man that You take thought of him, And the son of man that You care for him?[13]

Point 3:

If you are going to avoid conflict, then you must view your spouse as more important than you already see yourself.

What Should You do When You Find Yourself in Conflict?

You Must Guard Your Heart:

The heart is the control center of the inner man. It consists of your thoughts, intellect, reasoning, emotions, affections, will, and desires.[14]

Read the following scriptures and answer the questions below:

> Guard your heart above all else, for it determines the course of your life.[15]

12. Romans 12:3 (NASB)
13. Psalms 8:4 (NASB)
14. Proverbs 4:23 (NASB)
15. Proverbs 4:23 (NLT2)

1. What does it mean "to guard your heart?" _____
   _____
   _____

2. According to Proverbs 4:23, why do you need to "guard your heart?"
   _____
   _____

3. Are you called to guard your heart from what goes in, or from what comes out; why or Why not? (Clue: Matthew 15:18; Mark 7:17–23) __
   _____
   _____

   The heart is more deceitful than all else And is desperately sick;
   Who can understand it?[16]

4. What is wrong with your heart? _____
   _____
   _____

5. Can your heart be trusted? Is it a reliable source of truth; why or why not? _____
   _____
   _____

The primary responsibility of a corrections officer is to keep watch over prisoners. He monitors their offenders movements and takes note of any suspicious behaviors. His job is to make sure the offenders are secure as well as making sure he himself is protected from harm. He wants to make sure that those who are locked in a jail cell do not escape. He must make sure what is on the inside does not get out. For the prison guard to do his job well, he must stay alert and be watchful.

What does a prison guard have to do with your heart? You are the guard of your heart. During a conflict, the natural, sinful inclinations of your heart can rise up and attempt to escape. The offenders in your heart are unruly emotions, unloving attitudes, frustration, anger, cursing, deception, and evil thoughts. They all reside in your heart waiting for you to let your guard down so they can escape. Your job is to keep watch over them. You must be mindful of what is going on inside your heart. Be aware of behaviors that rise up within you that want to expose themselves through

16. Jeremiah 17:9 (NASB)

your flesh. You must be well-acquainted with their tendencies. No matter how difficult it may be, no matter how upset you are, stand firm under pressure. Don't give in. Stand your ground. Don't let them out! But do not rely solely on your own strength. You have an intercessor. He is the Holy Spirit. He is there to help, instruct, support, and sustain you. Listen to his voice and do what he is guiding you to do. The Holy Spirit tells you, don't say it, settle down, don't do it, stop, hold on, don't go there, God will not be pleased. You are under God's grace, so sin does not have control over you.[17]

What Should You Do When You Find Yourself in Conflict?

Not only must you guard your heart. You must exercise self-control.

> *Like* a city that is broken into *and* without walls Is a man who has no control over his spirit.[18]

Imagine what it would be like living life without the protection of walls. How many dangerous criminals would make a run for it if there were no prison walls? What would be the outcome if US Border Patrol ceased to exist, allowing anyone to enter our country unchecked?

In ancient times when a city was under the threat of being invaded, the city walls provided a fortress to keep the enemy out. Walls also prevented invaders from bringing horses in and stolen goods out. When a city was under attack and the walls were broken down, it left the city exposed and without protection, to be invaded and conquered by the enemy.

In Proverbs 25:28, Solomon compares an unfortified city under siege, whose walls have been broken down, to a man or woman who does not exercise self-control over his or her spirit. They leave themselves exposed. They have no control, reinforcement, or rule over their longings, cravings, and emotions. They allow their lust and anger to revolt against good character, moral judgment, and righteousness. They expose themselves to things that could destroy them physically, emotionally and spiritually. Here are some questions to consider:

1. What are some of the things that you crave? _____

_____

_____

17. Romans 6:14 (NASB)
18. Proverbs 25:28 (NASB)

2. What are some of your pleasures? _____

_____

_____

3. What are some of the emotions you experience when you are provoked to anger? _____

_____

_____

4. How do you respond when you have been offended by your spouse?

_____

_____

5. What are some of the temptations that you struggle with? _____

_____

_____

Food for Thought:

1. What would happen if you could no longer say "no" to the things that you crave? _____

_____

_____

2. What would be the outcome if you became a slave to your pleasures?

_____

_____

3. What would happen if you gave full vent to your anger? _____

_____

_____

4. What would happen if you exercised no restraints every time your spouse offended you? _____

_____

_____

5. What would happen if you yielded, without any level of resistance, to every form of temptation that came your way? _____

_____

_____

So is the fate of a man who has no control over his spirit!

> But each one [every man or woman] is tempted when he is carried away [broken into and without walls] and enticed by his lust [no control over his spirit, emotions, and passion]. Then when lust has conceived, it gives birth to sin; and when sin is accomplished, it brings forth death [destruction].[19]

A man who lacks self-control is on a road that leads to death. He will eventually experience self-destruction and ruin. His life will be shattered and torn down because his wall of protection is demolished. He not only destroys himself, but he destroys his relationship with others and harms other people.

How can you establish a wall to fortify your spirit when you are facing conflict with your spouse? When you are amid a dispute with your spouse, you must be aware of the fact that "every outbreaking of irritation, every spark of pride kindling in the heart, before it shows itself on the tongue, must be attacked and determinately resisted."[20] It is the beginning of a crack in your wall, and if it is not resolved quickly it will soon break, unleashing a tsunami of wrath and destruction. The aftermath could be quite costly—obedience to God's word is your wall of protection. But you cannot exercise obedience in your flesh. Self-control is only achievable by divine grace, through the power of the Holy Spirit.

The moment you recognize an attack, fortify your wall of protection and self-control by prayer. Prayer is acknowledging total dependence on the power of God for strength. Not only should you pray for yourself, but you must also pray for your spouse, recognizing that you are both sinners in need of grace, mercy, and forgiveness. Jesus, like we are, was tempted in many ways, yet he remained obedient.

> For we do not have a high priest who cannot sympathize with our weaknesses, but One who has been tempted in all things as *we are, yet* without sin.[21]

> He who is slow to anger is better than the mighty, And he who rules his spirit, than he who captures a city.[22]

---

19. James 1:14–15 (NASB)
20. Bridges, *A Commentary on Proverbs*, 483.
21. Hebrews 4:15 (NASB)
22. Proverbs 16:32 (NASB)

In the heat of a conflict, being mindful that prayer, obedience, and dependence upon the power of the Holy Spirit are essential to exercising self-control.

What Should You Do When You Find Yourself In Conflict?

You must guard your heart. You must exercise self-control.

You Must Control Your Tongue:

On Sunday mornings, the church is full of devoted Christian couples arriving for Sunday morning service. Some lift their hands in worship, pray eloquent prayers, carry big bibles, and serve in several ministries or leadership.

But a few of these same religious married couples will leave church, arrive home, and engage in a heated conflict using foul language that would make even the most perverted, cursing sailor cringe. How do I know? Because I have counseled some of them. There are people who consider themselves religious, devoted to serving and worshipping God, yet when they have no fear of being exposed by what others hear, they fail to control what comes out of their mouths.

> If anyone thinks himself to be religious, and yet does not bridle his tongue but deceives his *own* heart, this man's religion is worthless.[23]

1. What does the phrase, "if anyone thinks himself," mean? _____
_____
_____

2. What does it mean to "be religious?" _____
_____
_____

3. Do you consider yourself to be religious; why or why not? _____
_____
_____

23. James 1:26 (NASB)

4. James says in contrast to being a religious person is a man "who does not bridle his tongue." What are bridles used for, and how does it relate to your tongue? _____

_____

_____

5. What does it mean to "deceive" your own heart if you claim to be religious yet fail to control what comes out of your mouth? _____

_____

_____

6. What does it mean to have something in your possession that is "worthless?" _____

_____

_____

In chapter 5: Communication, we discussed the power of the tongue and how to avoid using it as an assault weapon against your spouse. If you find yourself in a conflict with your spouse and profess to be religious, saved, and sanctified, you must take responsibility for the words that come out of your mouth. Remember, the ability to control the tongue is not determined by feelings. Emotions and feelings are a product of the heart. As we already know, our hearts are deceitful and desperately wicked.[24] That means that our hearts are an unreliable source of truth, and it cannot be trusted. The heart lies against the truth to legitimize your feelings. The natural man is only concerned about himself.

Controlling the tongue is not based on feelings. It is an issue of choice. It is a matter of your determination to exhibit Christlikeness. It is a choice between succumbing to the desires of the flesh or exercising the religious commitment of pleasing, trusting, and worshiping God.

A bridle is a piece of equipment that is used to direct a horse. When the bit (mouthpiece) of the bridle is placed in a horse's mouth, the bridle can govern, restrain and direct the horse in any direction the rider desires. You bridle your tongue when you make a deliberate choice not to say what you want to say. You bridle your tongue when you direct your heart to steer away from thoughtless, hurtful, and corrupt words when you are tempted or provoked by your spouse. In truth, strength is not demonstrated by how well you can flex your verbal muscles but by your ability to restrain what comes out your mouth.

24. Jeremiah 17:9 (NASB)

I said, "I will watch my ways so that I will not sin with my tongue;
I will guard my mouth with a muzzle as long as the wicked are
present."[25]

What Should You Do When You Find Yourself in Conflict?

You must guard your heart. You must exercise self-control. You must control your tongue.

You Must Know When to Keep Silent:

Read the following verses and write down what they say about the value of keeping silent:

1. O that you would be completely silent, And that it would become your wisdom![26] _____
_____
_____

2. I said, "I will guard my ways That I may not sin with my tongue; I will guard my mouth as with a muzzle While the wicked are in my presence."[27] _____
_____
_____

3. When there are many words, transgression is unavoidable, But he who restrains his lips is wise.[28] _____
_____
_____

4. A fool's anger is known at once, But a prudent man conceals dishonor.[29] _____
_____
_____

25. Psalms 39:1 (NASB)
26. Job 13:5 (NASB)
27. Psalms 39:1 (NASB)
28. Proverbs 10:19 (NASB)
29. Proverbs 12:16 (NASB)

5. Starting a quarrel is like breaching a dam; so drop the matter before a dispute breaks out.[30] _____

_____

_____

6. He who restrains his words has knowledge, And he who has a cool spirit is a man of understanding. Even a fool, when he keeps silent, is considered wise; When he closes his lips, he is *considered* prudent.[31]

_____

_____

7. But I tell you that every careless word that people speak, they shall give an accounting for it in the day of judgment.[32] _____

_____

_____

8. For you have been called for this purpose, since Christ also suffered for you, leaving you an example for you to follow in His steps, who committed no sin, nor was any deceit found in his mouth; and while being reviled, He did not revile in return; while suffering, He uttered no threats, but kept entrusting *Himself* to Him who judges righteously[33]

_____

_____

9. How important is silence when your spouse is confrontational? _____

_____

_____

Among my most prized possessions are words that I have never spoken.[34]

If your spouse becomes belligerent during a conflict, you must keep silent. However, keep in mind that silence should not be lasting. Silence is a catalyst for allowing emotional tensions to settle down and cool off. Silence should not be used as a means of long-term avoidance, isolation, or as punishment. If you are keeping silent and distancing yourself from your spouse while entertaining anger, resentment, and bitterness, then your silence is sinfully fruitless.

30. Proverbs 17:14 (NIV)
31. Proverbs 17:27–28 (NASB)
32. Matthew 12:36 (NASB)
33. 1 Peter 2:21–23 (NASB)
34. Orson Scott Card, *BrainyQuote.com.*

Moreover, silence should never be used as a form of manipulation. Silence is to be used to deescalate the problem, to exercise wisdom, maintain self-control, and as a guard against yielding to the temptation to sin against your spouse. The goal is to calm the situation so that the issue can be resolved, at the appropriate time, in the proper manner.

What Should You Do When You Find Yourself in Conflict?

You must guard your heart. You must exercise self-control. You must control your tongue. You must know when to keep silent.

You Must Respond with Gentleness:

> A gentle answer turns away wrath, But a harsh word stirs up anger.[35]

A soft answer, response, or reply to something your spouse has said means to speak softly, tenderly, and gently. To be gentle means to handle with care in order to prevent breaking something fragile. A kind word is soft, not just in your choice of words, but it is mild in terms of your tone, as well as your delivery.

What is the effect of a gentle answer during a marital conflict? Proverbs 15:1 says it "turns away wrath." Wrath means hostility, anger, and rage. The first half of Proverbs 15:1 says that a gentle, soft, and tender reply to what your spouse says to you in a heated exchange will turn away, turn around, deflect heat, rage, anger, and hostility.

What are examples of gentle answers that you can say to your spouse during a conflict in order to turn away wrath? What are some kind words that are soft in terms of tone and delivery? If your spouse ever becomes angry, here are a few gentle responses you can use. If spoken just above a whisper it could turn away and calm the situation. Be mindful to avoid asking "why" questions because "why" generally causes people to become defensive:

- "What is your reason for being so upset?"

- "Tell me what you want from me at this moment."

- "How can I help and what is it that I am not doing?"

---

35. Proverbs 15:1 (NASB)

- "What have I done to offend you?"
- "My intent is not to hurt you in any way."
- "What can I do differently?"
- "How can I make it right?"
- "We simply do not see it the same, and that's okay—we are different."
- "Even though we disagree, know that I still love you."
- "I value your opinion. I appreciate you.
- "I am thankful that you are my husband or wife."

If you are at a lost regarding what to say during a conflict, you can ask your spouse what is the best way to calm them down when they are angry. Feel free to write your own response here: _____
_____
_____

But if you speak softly for more than five minutes and your spouse is still verbally expressing anger, then you must implement number four of this section—that is, you must know when to keep silent.

You might respond to this biblical principle with, "If I speak softly while my spouse is yelling, it will make him or her angrier!" You could be right, but not for long! If you continue to speak softly in response to a belligerent spouse, the angry spouse most often will eventually calm down. First, they come to realize they are talking much louder than you are. Second, they come to realize that they have lost control of themselves. Third, they may become convicted, feel guilty, and ashamed by how they are responding to the situation, circumstance, or event. The fact is, you cannot resolve conflict when you are angry. Both persons must deescalate.

Here is the caveat: After your spouse settles down, do not allow pride to rise within you and reignite the argument. After things have calmed down do not remind yourself of all the harsh words said by your angry spouse and decide that you will not let him or her off the hook for speaking to you in that manner. If you decide to confront him or her right after a heated situation has calmed down, you will be right back where you started. Do not let pride cause you to strike a match after the flame has been put out. Pray for God's wisdom about when to confront wrong behavior and when to remain silent.

> For the lord gives wisdom; from his mouth come knowledge and understanding; he stores up sound wisdom for the upright; he is a shield to those who walk in integrity, guarding the paths of justice . . . discretion will watch over you . . . understanding will guard you, delivering you from the way of evil, from men of perverted speech[36]

When you are attempting to give a gentle answer, you must avoid asking "why" questions because "why" generally causes people to become defensive. If you ask your spouse why she did that, why he said this, or why did he or she make that decision, you are really asking them to justify their actions. They will immediately assume, often rightly so, that you do not approve of their actions or decisions. Therefore, they respond from a defensive position.

Also, avoid using words such as "you always" or "you never." Always and never are usually not true statements and indicate extreme exaggeration. Also avoid using "but you" and "if you." Spouses will sometimes use "but you" and "if you" when they are attempting to justify their actions and wrong behavior.

Proverbs 15:1 also says, "But a harsh word stirs up anger." A harsh word does just the opposite of a gentle answer. The word "harsh" is not merely referring to rudeness, although it includes it. The word harsh refers to words spoken that cause emotional pain to the recipient. Harsh words hurt and injure the other person. You and your spouse are well-acquainted with one another's weaknesses, struggles, and failures. During a conflict, you may be tempted to use what you know about each other as an arsenal. Screaming, yelling, cursing your spouse, name-calling, and using sarcasm can be received as harsh. So, a harsh word, reply, or response is one that hits below the belt. It is similar to throwing a knockout punch in a boxing ring. Once a boxer is wounded, the opponent now targets the place of injury, whether it is a small cut above the eye, a blow to the body, or a broken rib. His goal is to bring down his opponent, preferably by way of knockout. Sometimes in a heated argument, couples will use harsh words to attack the place of injury to bring down their opposing spouse by way of knockout.

Unlike a gentle answer that turns away wrath, a harsh, painful word stirs up anger. The term "anger" literally means to flare the nostrils, similar to a dog who flares his nose and flashes his teeth before attacking. The word "stir up" means to move in an upward direction. It denotes an ascension to a higher place. Instead of deflecting wrath, a harsh word invites anger

36. Proverbs 2:6–8, 11–12 (NASB)

in and then stirs it up like a pot of hot soup brewing in a pressure cooker. In reality, a harsh, painful word takes tempers to a higher place. Can you imagine firefighters arriving at your house attempting to put out a fire by dousing it with gasoline? A one-alarm fire has now become a three-alarm blaze. The fire has been magnified and escalated to another destructive level—so it is when you use harsh words during a conflict with your spouse. It takes anger to another level that may result in spiritual and emotional casualties. The damage can be so significant that it may become tough for either of you to recover.

1. Ask your spouse for some examples of harsh words that you need to avoid using during conflict that end up stirring up anger. What are words that you know are your spouse's "hot buttons?" _____

    _____
    _____

2. What are you going to do going forward to turn away wrath? _____

    _____
    _____

What Should You Do When You Find Yourself in Conflict?

You must guard your heart. You must exercise self-control. You must control your tongue. You must know when to keep silent. You must respond with gentleness.

What Should You do After a Conflict has Already Occurred?

Many times, couples are reluctant to take the initiative to make right a wrong after a conflict or heated argument has taken place. They spend time pouting or giving one another the silent treatment that may last for days. Each person is pressing the rewind button in their minds, rehearsing the harsh, cruel words that the other person said. As they do so, their emotions are being stirred up, and wounds are being reopened. Each is focusing on how they have been mistreated and offended. Each of them is pointing the finger at the other person because they see the other person as the problem and not themselves. They fail to take the time to consider what they have done to contribute to the problem and the harsh words that they used to attack their spouse during the conflict.

When they think of their actions, frequently they will always make attempts to either justify, deny, or ignore their sinful behavior (words, deeds, and attitudes). Each spouse is selfishly and pridefully sitting, watching, and waiting for the other person to admit they are wrong and take the initiative to make amends. Will this kind of behavior restore a marriage after a conflict has occurred? No. Will this bring about unity and peace to the home? Is this kind of behavior between husband and wife pleasing to the Lord? No! Then what needs to happen? What should you do after a conflict has already occurred? Where do you start?

You must realize that sometimes, during the conflict, your spouse may seem as if they have become your worst enemy. If you allow unresolved conflict to linger, you and your spouse will begin to live as strangers living in the same home. The reason is that you are both functioning out of selfishness and empty conceit. It is all about you, what you want, how you have been offended, and what you are not getting from the other person. Your attitude is not necessarily for the betterment of the marriage but self-gratification. Before salvation, you and your spouse were enemies of God. Worthy of his wrath and death. So, how did God restore a broken relationship with sinful humanity?

> Have this attitude in yourselves which was also in Christ Jesus, who, although He existed in the form of God, did not regard equality with God a thing to be grasped, but emptied Himself, taking the form of a bond-servant, *and* being made in the likeness of men. Being found in appearance as a man, by becoming obedient to the point of death, even death on a cross.[37]

God loved you so much that he sent Jesus to die to pay the penalty for your sins. Jesus Christ, the King of Kings and Lord of Lords, humbled Himself and committed to obedience to the will of the Father, all the way to the cross. As a result, a severed relationship with man is restored to all those who have faith in the person and work of Jesus Christ. Jesus Christ is the perfect picture of God's love, demonstrated by humility, sacrifice, and giving.

If you want to restore your relationship with your spouse after a conflict has occurred, you must exemplify the character of Christ. How? You must realize that your purpose in life is to glorify God.

---

37. Philippians 2:5–8 (NASB)

> Therefore, we also have as our ambition, whether at home or absent, to be pleasing to Him.[38]

So, as we discuss the solution to the conflict, always keep in mind that your ambition, your goal in life is to glorify the Lord. But you may ask, "what does it mean to glorify God" or "How can I please Him?" Scripture says that everything that happens to us, including conflict, works together for the good of those who love God, to conform us to the image of Christ.[39] The fact is, we are like Christ in position the moment we declared faith in Jesus Christ. We are justified by his blood. However, God wants us to conform to the image of his son in practice in terms of how we relate to others and live our lives.

As you consider Jesus's life on earth, what kind of person is he?

1. How did he relate to people in need? Be specific: _____
   _____
   _____

2. What did Jesus specifically do the help others? _____
   _____
   _____

3. How many people, whom he helped, actually said "thank you?" _____
   _____
   _____

4. How did Jesus respond to his enemies? _____
   _____
   _____

5. What was Jesus motivation for relating to people the way that he did?
   _____
   _____

6. Jesus came to the do the will of the father, to glorify him and to do his will! So how can you glorify the Father? _____
   _____
   _____

---

38. 2 Corinthians 5:9 (NASB)
39. Romans 8:28–29 (NASB)

> And now, Israel, what does the lord your God require of you, but to fear the lord your God, to walk in all his ways, to love him, to serve the lord your God with all your heart and with all your soul[40]

The command to love God and others captures the essence of what it means to reflect the image of Christlikeness and to glorify God. So, as it relates to marriage, the evidence of your love for God can be seen by how well you demonstrate unconditional love for your spouse, especially during conflict. Loving like Jesus is shown through sacrifice, giving, doing good, and expecting nothing in return.

What Should You Do After A Conflict Has Already Occurred?

You must realize that your purpose in life is to glorify God.

You Must Recognize the Good in Conflict:

> And we know that God causes all things to work together for good to those who love God, to those who are called according to *His* purpose.[41]

God can use conflict to purge you and your spouse so that the impurities of your hearts are exposed to purify and perfect your marriage. The result is a marriage that is a reflection of his image, an image of unity of plurality (Father, Son, and the Holy Spirit) and singular (one true God) at the same time, as well as an image of his communicable attributes of unconditional love, grace, mercy, goodness, forgiveness, patience, and long-suffering.

How can you identify the impurities of your heart?

They can be determined by what you say!

> The good man out of the good treasure of his heart brings forth what is good; the evil *man* out of the evil *treasure* brings forth what is evil; for his mouth speaks from that which fills his heart.[42]

---

40. Deuteronomy 10:12 (ESV)
41. Romans 8:28 (NASB)
42. Luke 6:45 (NASB)

It is relatively easy to hide the issues of your heart when you are in public. You risk sabotaging your reputation and exposing your true character. But, it is challenging to do the same when you are angry with your spouse because there is not much risk of ruining your reputation, so all filters are gone and the true proclivities of your heart flow out. The truth is when most of us are angry it is a challenge to restrain our hearts. Conflict exposes the heart. Read on to learn what you should do after your heart is exposed.

You must reflect on what transpired during the conflict and take time to evaluate yourself by asking yourself:

- Were my words, attitude, and responses sinful against my spouse?
- Were my words displeasing in God's sight?
- Was I honest with my spouse?
- Is my spouse right about what they said, not necessarily in tone but in content?
- Am I harboring bitterness, resentment, and hatred?
- Am I prideful?
- Am I all about self?

If you answered yes to any of the above, then you have successfully identified some of your heart issues. You may be tempted to ask, "What good is there in identifying my heart issues?" There is always hope for spiritual growth and change when a person can see themselves from God's perspective. When you do, you can commit to making changes in your life. Your heart issues are confession points. Change involves confession, seeking forgiveness from God and your spouse, and then repentance. Conflict is an excellent opportunity for personal spiritual growth and for perfecting the marriage.

What Should You Do After A Conflict Has Already Occurred?

You must realize that your purpose in life is to glorify God. You must recognize the good in conflict. You must evaluate yourself and confess your heart issues.

You Must Take the Initiative to Make Peace with Your Spouse:

> So then, we pursue the things which make for peace and the building up of one another.[43]

If you ask a person who does things out selfishness and empty conceit to take the initiative to make peace with their spouse, they will probably respond with, "Why should I be the first one to apologize? He wronged me first. Let her come to me! Until then, I am not budging!" Where there is no peace, there is disorder and every evil thing.[44] Taking the initiative to be the first to approach your spouse in seeking peace requires humility, especially when you believe your spouse is wrong. Pursuing peace with others, especially your spouse, is not a suggestion but a command. It finds favor with God when you take the initiative to seek reconciliation after being mistreated.

> For this *finds* favor if for the sake of conscience toward God a person bears up under sorrows when suffering unjustly.[45]

> If possible, so far as it depends on you, be at peace with all men.[46]

What Should You Do After A Conflict Has Already Occurred?

You must realize that your purpose in life is to glorify God. You must recognize the good in Conflict. You must evaluate yourself and confess your heart issues. You must take the initiative to make peace with your spouse.

You Must Seek to Restore Your Spouse:

> Brethren, even if anyone is caught in any trespass, you who are spiritual, restore such a one in a spirit of gentleness; *each one* looking to yourself, so that you too will not be tempted.[47]

43. Romans 14:19 (NASB)
44. James 3:16 (NASB)
45. 1 Peter 2:19 (NASB)
46. Romans 12:18 (NASB)
47. Galatians 6:1 (NASB)

"Brethren" is the first word in Galatians 6:1. The term "brethren" refers to those who are believers in Christ. If you are a believer in Christ, then "brethren" includes you. The writer then says if anyone of your brothers and sisters in Christ succumbs to sin in general, you have a responsibility to exercise spiritual maturity and restore them. During a conflict, either of you at any point during the battle has been guilty of being overcome by unloving words, attitudes, and sinful actions. Since you and your spouse are also brother and sister in Christ, you should restore one another in a spirit of humility.

The word "restore" means to make wrongs right, to repair or mend that which is broken. As you do so, you must be mindful of your propensity to sin. You must be aware of your inadequacies, temptations, and failures. You are capable of committing the same sin or worse sins than those of your spouse, but the same grace and mercy that covers your sin is the same grace and mercy that covers his or hers. After a conflict, seek to restore your spouse by exercising spiritual maturity and pursuing restoration in a spirit of humility with self-awareness. Real restoration can only occur by seeking and granting forgiveness.

> For if you forgive others for their transgressions, your heavenly Father will also forgive you. But if you do not forgive others, then your Father will not forgive your transgressions.[48]

What Should You Do After A Conflict Has Already Occurred?

You must realize that your purpose in life is to glorify God. You must recognize the good in conflict. You must evaluate yourself and confess your heart issues. You must take the initiative to make peace with your spouse. You must seek to restore your spouse.

You Must Show Concern for the Interest of Your Spouse:

Let's go back and discuss the rest of the Scripture we used in the introduction of this chapter.

> Do nothing from selfishness or empty conceit, but with humility of mind regard one another as more important than yourselves; do

---

48. Matthew 6:14–15 (NASB)

not *merely* look out for your own personal interests, but also for the interests of others.[49]

Paul says we should put the interest of others before our own. Your interests consist of non-material things that you desire, want, expect, and need from your spouse. They are things that your spouse is in possession of and has the ability to give and satisfy. How does this apply to marital conflict resolution? Look at it this way: You have needs. I have needs. We all have personal interests and things that we desire. We view these things as meaningful to us. Paul says in Philippians that no matter how important you think your interests are, you are to consider the interests of others as equally or more important than your own. Conflict resolution is achievable when you and your spouse view and value one another's interests, desires, and needs as more important than your own.

When you place your spouse first before yourself, you can avoid unnecessary conflict. Conflict resolution involves the unconditional love of Christ that is demonstrated by sacrifice and giving. When both husband and wife are exhibiting love in this manner, then they have the unity of oneness void of ungodly conflict. If you and your spouse are joint heirs in Christ, then you are to live in harmony with one another. Live in fellowship, with compassion and affection for one another, humility of mind, and walking side by side through life together, despite your differences and unmet expectations. Sometimes you have to endure suffering as a result of conflict, out of your love for God and your spouse. Your purpose in life is to please God.

> Therefore if there is any encouragement in Christ, if there is any consolation of love, if there is any fellowship of the Spirit, if any affection and compassion, make my joy complete by being of the same mind, maintaining the same love, united in spirit, intent on one purpose.[50]

What Should You Do After A Conflict Has Already Occurred?

You must realize that your purpose in life is to glorify God. You must recognize the good in conflict. You must evaluate yourself and confess your heart issues. You must take the initiative to make peace with your Spouse. You

49. Philippians 2:3–4 (NASB)
50. Philippians 2:1–2 (NASB)

must seek to restore your spouse. You must show concern for the interest of your spouse.

Conclusion:

The sinful desires of our flesh are the source of conflict. It stems from an unbiblical response to not getting what we want or when we are getting words, actions, and behavior from others we do not want, even if they are with wrong or right intentions. However, as believers, our goal in life is to be pleasing to God. You can only please God when you conform to the image of his son.

The solution to marital conflict is to have the mind, actions, and attitude of Christ. The Apostle Paul said in Philippians 2:3–4 that you are to do nothing from selfishness and vainglory that causes contention in relationships. He also said you are to exhibit humility by regarding others as more important than yourself. Then Apostle Paul drives home his point with the following verse:

> Have this attitude in yourselves which was also in Christ Jesus[51]

What does conforming to the image of Christ look like in your marriage? It is an image that displays the love of God, evidenced by loving your spouse unconditionally. It is a love that is not driven by what your spouse can do for you. Selfish demands or personal pleasures do not facilitate unity. The mind, action, and attitude of Christ are one of humility. Therefore, the solution to conflict is exhibiting the mind of Christ. It involves being merciful when you believe that your spouse deserves judgment. The answer to conflict is giving your spouse grace and unmerited favor even when they do not deserve it. The solution to conflict means forgiveness, patience, loving-kindness, long-suffering, goodness, and gentleness. The solution to conflict is taking the initiative to make wrongs right. It is exhibiting love (*agape*), the highest love, selfless, sacrificial, unconditional love that covers a multitude of sins. The solution for conflict is to pursue peace with your spouse for the glory of God. It is a commitment to your spouse, determined not to allow anything to cause disunity and disharmony in your relationship. It requires refraining from living a feeling-oriented life of sin and pursuing a commandment-oriented life geared towards glorifying God.

---

51. Philippians 2:5 (NASB)

When you experience conflict with your spouse, my challenge to you is to make the same commitment that King David made when he said, "I will guard my ways That I may not sin with my tongue; I will guard my mouth as with a muzzle While the wicked are in my presence."[52]

Here is a daily prayer for you and your spouse:

Lord,

Please forgive me for the sinful attitudes, words, and actions during conflict that have offended you, as well as those that I exhibit towards my spouse. Lord, give me the mind of Christ to do nothing from selfishness or empty conceit, but with humility of mind show me how to regard my spouse as more important than myself. Help me to deny self and not to *merely* look out for my own personal interests but also for the concerns of my spouse. I pray Lord, through the power of the Holy Spirit, that you help me to let all bitterness and wrath and anger and clamor and slander be put away from me, along with all malice. Help me and my spouse to be kind to one another, tender-hearted, and forgiving of each other, just as God in Christ also has forgiven us. And I will be careful to give you all the glory and praise due your name. In the Name of Jesus, I pray. Amen!

Conflict Resolution Application Homework:

Quiz: Contention, Selfishness, and Vain Glory:

Rate yourself and your spouse by entering 0 = never, 1 = rarely, 2 = sometimes, 3 = almost always, and 4 = always, in each of the respective columns for each of the following statements. Give an example or brief explanation for each answer that is a "3" or "4."

Statement:	Him:	Her:	Example/Explanation:
1. I am quick to argue.			

---

52. Psalms 39:1 (NASB)

Statement:	Him:	Her:	Example/Explanation:
2. I am strongly opinionated.			
3. I become angry when my spouse disagrees with me.			
4. I become upset when things are unorganized.			
5. My way of doing things is the right way.			
6. I become upset when I feel my spouse does not appreciate me.			
7. I am slow to admit when I am wrong.			
Score:			

If your score is 0 to 7, you rarely have conflict; 8 to 14, sometimes experience conflict; 15 to 21 always in conflict; if it is 22 to 28, you can't even talk without conflict.

How Can You Exercise Humility?

Define the following keywords, insert "Y" for those character traits you believe you exhibit and an "N" for those areas where you think you need improvement. Schedule time with your spouse to review and compare your answers. Then ask your spouse if he or she agrees with your answers and why or why not. Finally, ask your spouse for specific practical ways you can make improvements in the areas where you struggle.

Keyword:	Keyword defined as:	Do I relate to my spouse with (insert keyword)?	If not, what will I do to improve in this area?
Humility:			
Gentleness:			
Patience:			

Keyword:	Keyword defined as:	Do I relate to my spouse with (insert keyword)?	If not, what will I do to improve in this area?
Tolerance:			
Love:			
A desire to maintain unity:			
Being peace-able:			

9

Intimacy that Equates to Oneness

Love, Sex, Romance, and Companionship

Counseling Issue:

JERRY AND ANNIE ARE newlyweds. They have been married for six months and are beginning to experience marital problems. The love they once felt for one another seems to have vanished. The physical, emotional, mental, and spiritual intimacy that previously took residence in their hearts appears to have packed its bags and left. Here are some of their issues:

- Whenever Jerry wants to have sex, it seems that Annie is never in the mood.

- Annie feels that Jerry is insensitive to her needs and does not seem to care when she makes attempts to share her feelings. Jerry says he does not like drama and that Annie is too emotional about everything.

- Jerry is bothered that Annie seeks the advice of her father rather than coming to him.

- Annie is frustrated because Jerry puts everything before her. They spend no quality time together, and there is no romance in the relationship. For Jerry, planning for her birthday, Valentine's day, and special occasions is an afterthought, Annie says.

- Their differing opinions always turn into arguments.

- They have separate checking accounts and disputes about money.

- Jerry has a problem with some of Annie's friends, especially those of the opposite sex. Annie believes having opposite-sex friends should not be an issue since they were her friends and colleagues before she met Jerry.
- Annie is heavily involved in church, but Jerry is inconsistent in his church attendance and would rather stay home on Sunday and watch football games.

The Problem:

The main issue associated with the problems that Jerry and Annie are experiencing is the lack of intimacy. They have disconnected physically from the lack of sex. Jerry has detached emotionally by being insensitive to Annie's feelings. They are experiencing a mental disconnect because their prideful attitudes have led each to believe that their individual opinion is the only one that matters.

They are embracing individualism, the belief that "what's mine is mine, and what's yours is yours." Annie maintains relationships with opposite-sex friends that could potentially cause division in the marriage. Impetuously, opposite-sex friends could become pillars to lean on when you are experiencing a problem with your spouse. This creates a vulnerable situation that places you at risk. Finally, Jerry and Annie are spiritually disjointed. It appears that they are moving in opposite directions as it relates to the importance of worshiping God and serving in ministry work.

So, where do you begin to reconcile a relationship that is void of intimacy? Is there any hope for a marriage where there is a severe disconnect? How can Jerry and Annie rekindle and restore the flame that they once had for one another when they first said, "I do?" There is always hope for those in Christ Jesus.

Objective:

The purpose of this chapter is to help couples avoid the misery of a marriage that lacks true intimacy, to understand, establish, and maintain intimacy through the exercising of oneness in every area of their marriage.

Marriage was created to reflect the image of God. Therefore, marriage is a covenant of companionship, where both the husband and wife are living as one. As such, the focus of this chapter will be to help couples learn how to practically experience physical, emotional, mental, and spiritual intimacy in a way that allows love, peace, joy, and harmony to permeate their marriage and bring honor and glory to God.

Marital Intimacy:

God created male and female to reflect his image. They are to be joined in holy matrimony and the two are to become one flesh. Marriage is designed to be monogamous and heterosexual. It is the complete union of two people. Husbands and wives are to live dependent on one another, and without separate rights, privileges, and prerogatives. They are to cherish one another, love one another, and embrace one another. A husband and wife must view their marriage and one another as the most important thing above all other relationships, except for their relationship with God. Their relationship to one another is their priority, and it is designed to be permanent.

> The man said, "This is now bone of my bones, And flesh of my flesh; She shall be called Woman, Because she was taken out of Man." For this reason a man shall leave his father and his mother, and be joined to his wife; and they shall become one flesh.[1]

> I and the Father are one.[2]

There is nothing more demonstrative of male and female becoming one flesh than what can be seen when you look into the face of a child. Usually, a child has facial features that resemble both parents. She may have her father's eyes and her mother's nose. Some people may say she looks more like her father. Others may disagree and swear that she looks like her mother.

In some cases, a child may bear features that only resemble one parent. But as the child grows older, her facial features began to change to those that most resemble the other parent. The child is the life, flesh, and bone produced out of two becoming one flesh, but babies are not all that is produced. Sexual intimacy also produces a profound emotional, mental, and spiritual oneness between a man and a woman.

1. Genesis 2:23–24 (NASB)
2. John 10:30 (NASB)

You cannot establish oneness without intimacy. Intimacy plays a vital role in experiencing oneness. Even if a man engages in sexual intercourse with a woman that he is not married to, he is still one with her. He is one with her in terms of union, not marriage. The Apostle Paul wrote: "Or do you not know that the one who joins himself to a prostitute is one body with her? For He says, '*The two shall become one flesh*'"[3]

When a man thinks of intimacy the first thing that usually comes to mind is sex. But genuine affection involves much more than sex. The word "intimacy" is defined as a close, familiar, and usually affectionate or loving personal relationship with another person. It involves a detailed knowledge or deep understanding of someone or something.[4] Synonyms for intimacy include closeness, warmth, familiarity, affection, inseparability, nearness, and belonging. When a couple is intimate, they experience emotional closeness, connectedness, and affection toward one another. There is a sense of nearness and belonging in the marriage. When a husband and wife exhibit intimacy, they appear inseparable. So, what does real intimacy look like in practice? Let us take a moment to examine the following paths for establishing intimacy.

Physical Intimacy:

Physical intimacy, in general, occurs when a husband and wife are physically connected. Each person welcomes the other into their personal space. They enjoy being in proximity to each other.

1. With the exception of sex, give some examples of how couples can exhibit physical intimacy with one another. _____
   _____
   _____

2. Which expressions of physical intimacy do you enjoy most and why?
   _____   _____
   _____

3. What expressions of physical intimacy do you believe your spouse or fiancée would enjoy most and why? _____

---

3. 1 Corinthians 6:16 (NASB)
4. "Intimacy." Collins English Dictionary.

Regardless of your personal preference as it relates to physical intimacy, there are benefits when couples engage one another. Read the following Scripture and list all the benefits of physical intimacy and togetherness. ____

> Two are better than one because they have a good return for their labor. For if either of them falls, the one will lift up his companion. But woe to the one who falls when there is not another to lift him up. Furthermore, if two lie down together they keep warm, but how can one be warm alone? And if one can overpower him who is alone, two can resist him. A cord of three strands is not quickly torn apart.[5]

Sexual Intimacy:

Sex is another avenue of physical intimacy. From the world's perspective, sex is a means by which one can use another person's body for personal pleasure and self-gratification. Many people get married so that they can enjoy as much sex as possible. The world views sex as a means for personal fulfillment. In other words, the goal of having sex is not always about the giving of oneself to another for their enjoyment. Sex is mostly about taking and using the body of another for personal pleasure. In some cases, those who have no restraints when it comes to seeking avenues for sexual fulfillment end up being caught in a downward spiral of sexual idolatry, driven by an insatiable lust. The flesh is never satisfied.

> The appetite of the flesh is never satisfied. It is like the stomach. No matter how much you feed it today, it always comes back tomorrow, wanting more.[6]

But from a biblical perspective, the purpose of sex is not about taking and using the body of another for personal pleasure. Sex is about giving of yourself to your spouse for *their* enjoyment as an open expression of love.

5. Ecclesiastes 4:9–12 (NASB)
6. Solzhenitsyn, *One Day*.

The husband is seeking to satisfy his wife first before himself, and the wife tries to please her husband. In doing so, both husband and wife are to give and receive the utmost pleasure from one another. Husbands and wives have a biblical obligation to offer themselves to each other sexually.

Sexual unity in marriage is not only pleasurable, but it is therapeutic, soothing, and comforting. Moreover, sex is a sincere expression of genuine love between a husband and a wife. Sexual intimacy can be a measuring rod that reflects the condition of the marriage. In many cases, when a couple is experiencing disunity for an extended length of time, they more than likely have also disconnected sexually.

How important is sex in marriage? Read the following text and answer the corresponding questions:

> Marriage is to be held in honor among all, and the marriage bed is to be undefiled; for fornicators and adulterers God will judge.[7]

1. Hebrews 13:4 says that the "marriage is to be held in honor among all." What does it mean to honor something? _____
   _____
   _____

2. At a wedding ceremony, in what ways do people show that marriage is honored? _____
   _____
   _____

3. Hebrews 13:4 says that we ought to celebrate the marriage union, and that "the marriage bed is to be undefiled." The marriage bed refers to sexual activity, where the husband and wife are enjoying one another totally without inhibition, reluctance, or discomfort—and it is undefiled. What does the word "undefiled" mean? _____
   _____
   ____ _____

4. If the marriage bed is honorable, reputable, wholesome, virtuous, and moral, what defiles the marriage bed? Clue: "for fornicators and adulterers God will judge"[8] _____
   _____
   _____

7. Hebrews 13:4 (NASB)
8. Hebrews 13:4 (NASB)

Note:

Any form of sexual immorality can also defile the marriage bed. Sexual immorality refers to all illicit sexual activity apart from marriage. Sexual immorality, in the New Testament in the Greek word, *porneia*. It is where we get the word pornography. Sexual immorality involves any form of evil, lewd, and perverted sexual activity, particularly apart from marriage. However, marriage partners are not to induce and entertain sexual acts into the marriage bed that both husband and wife are not entirely comfortable in doing, or something that may cause harm.

> Do not deprive each other of sexual relations unless you both agree to refrain from sexual intimacy for a limited time so you can give yourselves more completely to prayer. Afterward, you should come together again so that Satan will not be able to tempt you because of your lack of self-control.[9]

1. What does 1 Corinthians 7:5 say about withholding sex from your spouse? _____
   _____
   _____

2. In what ways do some people make attempts to misuse and abuse the principle of 1 Corinthians 7:5? _____
   _____
   _____

3. In what instances is withholding sex from your spouse permissible and what should be the purpose? _____
   _____
   _____

> The husband must fulfill his duty to his wife, and likewise also the wife to her husband. The wife does not have authority over her own body, but the husband does; and likewise also the husband does not have authority over his own body, but the wife does.[10]

9. 1 Corinthians 7:5 (NLT2)
10. 1 Corinthians 7:3–4 (NASB)

1. According to 1 Corinthians 7:3, what is the husband's and wife's responsibility to one another? What do you need to know to fulfill your duty? _____

_____

_____

2. In Corinthians 7:4, What does it mean to have authority over your spouse's body? _____

_____

_____

3. In what ways can 1 Corinthians 7:3–4 be abused and misused? _____

_____

_____

When couples engage in sexual unity, they are also engaging with one another, emotionally, mentally, and spiritually. Physical and sexual intimacy is a means by which a husband and wife can cleave to one another.

Emotional Intimacy:

Emotional intimacy occurs when you and your spouse or fiancé develop a deep knowledge and affection for one another. You become emotionally connected with your partner when you feel what they feel, hurt when they hurt, and rejoice when they rejoice. When you are emotionally connected with the other person, you can discern an issue or problem without the other person saying a word. An emotionally connected couple will know what brings joy, delight, fear, anxiety, hurt, and stress upon their spouse and can offer comfort and encouragement in times of emotional need.

Read 1 Peter 3:8 and define the following key terms in the text and give a practical example of each:

> To sum up, all of you be harmonious, sympathetic, brotherly, kindhearted, and humble in spirit[11]

1. Harmonious: _____

_____

_____

11. 1 Peter 3:8 (NASB)

Practical example: _____

_____

_____

2. Sympathetic: _____

_____

_____

Practical example: _____

_____

_____

3. Brotherly or sisterly: _____

_____

_____

Practical example: _____

_____

_____

4. Kindhearted: _____

_____

_____

Practical example: _____

_____

_____

Here are some other examples of how couples can experience emotional intimacy. Circle the ones that you would enjoy the most and compare your answers with your spouse or fiancée's answers:

Him:	Her:
Having casual conversations.	Having casual conversations.
Talking and texting throughout the day.	Talking and texting throughout the day.

Him:	Her:
Listening to my concerns without being judgmental.	Listening to my concerns without being judgmental.
Being able to share where I hurt.	Being able to share where I hurt.
Receiving grace when I make a mistake.	Receiving grace when I make a mistake.
Spending quality time together.	Spending quality time together.
Romance or having date nights.	Romance or having date nights.
Feeling that my spouse understands me.	Feeling that my spouse understands me.
Showing appreciation for what I do.	Showing appreciation for what I do.
Gentle correction when I am wrong.	Gentle correction when I am wrong.
Thinking well of and complimenting me often.	Thinking well of and complimenting me often.
Holding each other.	Holding each other.
Laughing together.	Laughing together.

Mental Intimacy:

Mental intimacy happens when you and your spouse become united in heart and mind. It involves the exchange of thoughts and ideas. Intellectual intimacy occurs when you and your spouse share knowledge, presuppositions, ideologies, theories, speculations, and doctrine. It is a delightful thing when you can freely share what you think and care about with the one you love. Mental intimacy also involves the ability to share your thoughts openly with your spouse about life in general: your dreams, desires, places you would like to go, things you'd like to do, and future goals. It occurs when each person values the thoughts, interests, and ideas of the other person more than their own without competition. It requires sacrifice, and sacrifice is always demonstrated through giving and listening. When you accept and respect your differences in ideas, thoughts, and opinions, without irritation and contention, then you are engaging in mental intimacy.

Most importantly, mental intimacy requires having the mind of Christ. When you and your spouse exhibit the mind of Christ, you create a loving atmosphere of mutual and mental intimacy that is demonstrated by loving one another even when you do not see eye-to-eye. It produces unity, peace, and harmony in the marital relationship.

What does it mean to have the mind of Christ? Read the following Scripture and write down what each says about having the mind of Christ.

> Therefore if there is any encouragement in Christ, if there is any consolation of love, if there is any fellowship of the Spirit, if any affection and compassion, make my joy complete by being of the same mind, maintaining the same love, united in spirit, intent on one purpose.[12]

_____

_____

> Do nothing from selfishness or empty conceit, but with humility of mind regard one another as more important than yourselves; do not merely look out for your own personal interests, but also for the interests of others.[13]

_____

_____

12. Philippians 2:1–2 (NASB)
13. Philippians 2:3–4 (NASB)

Have this attitude in yourselves which was also in Christ Jesus, who, although He existed in the form of God, did not regard equality with God a thing to be grasped[14]

_____

_____

but emptied Himself, taking the form of a bond-servant, and being made in the likeness of men. Being found in appearance as a man, He humbled Himself by becoming obedient to the point of death, even death on a cross.[15]

_____

_____

Be of the same mind toward one another; do not be haughty in mind, but associate with the lowly. Do not be wise in your own estimation.[16]

_____

_____

Based upon your observations from the previous Scriptures regarding the mind of Christ, what do you believe causes disruption or hinders mental intimacy in a marriage relationship? _____

_____

_____

Mental intimacy requires having the mind of Christ:

- Humility: lowliness of spirit.
- Sacrifice: giving.
- Obedience to God: a desire and ambition to please God.
- Valuing your spouse as more important than yourself.

14. Philippians 2:5–6 (NASB)
15. Philippians 2:7–8 (NASB)
16. Romans 12:16 (NASB)

As you ponder these four characteristics that summarize the mind of Christ, please answer the following questions:

1. What is the opposite of humility? _____
   _____
   _____

2. What is the opposite of sacrifice? _____
   _____
   _____

3. What would you call a person who refuses to obey God? _____
   _____
   _____

4. What would you call a person who is more concerned about themselves than they are their spouse? _____
   _____
   _____

Are you exhibiting the mind of Christ? If not, what are you going to do to improve? Make a list of changes you are going to make and pray.

> Finally, brethren, rejoice, be made complete, be comforted, be like-minded, live in peace; and the God of love and peace will be with you.[17]

Spiritual Intimacy:

Spiritual intimacy occurs when a husband and wife are united in Christ and in spirit. As a result of being united in Christ, husbands and wives are to strive together in life, hand in hand, pursuing one purpose, one goal, and one ambition. What is your purpose in life? What should be your ambition and your ultimate goal?

Your mission and goal in life is to have a marriage that reflects the image of God, where both you and your spouse are striving to live a life pleasing to God by growing in the likeness of Jesus Christ, by exercising obedience, humility, and a genuine love for God, one another, and others.

Spiritual Intimacy takes place when both the husband and wife are:

17. 2 Corinthians 13:11 (NASB)

- Reflecting God's image: "God created man in His own image, in the image of God He created him; male and female He created them."[18]

- Committed to pleasing God: "Therefore we also have as our ambition, whether at home or absent, to be pleasing to Him."[19]

- Growing in the likeness in Christ: "And we know that God causes all things to work together for good to those who love God, to those who are called according to His purpose. For those whom He foreknew, He also predestined to become conformed to the image of His Son, so that He would be the firstborn among many brethren"[20]

Read the following Scriptures and answer the corresponding questions:

> Only conduct yourselves in a manner worthy of the gospel of Christ, so that whether I come and see you or remain absent, I will hear of you that you are standing firm in one spirit, with one mind striving together for the faith of the gospel[21]

1. The phrase, "conduct yourselves," means to live as a citizen. Conduct has to do with one's behavior. How are you to conduct yourselves? ____

   _____

   _____

2. Paul says believers should stand firm in one spirit which is essential to Christian conduct whose citizenship is in Heaven. Often soldiers stand firm together, no matter how severe the battle. What does it mean to stand firm in "one spirit"? _____

   _____

   _____

3. Why is unity of mind, soul, and spirit so important as a couple is striving together in faith as they seek to reflect God's image, glorify God, grow in Christ, and share the gospel? _____

   _____

   _____

18. Genesis 1:27 (NASB)
19. 2 Corinthians 5:9 (NASB)
20. Romans 8:28–29 (NASB)
21. Philippians 1:27 (NASB)

Incentives for Seeking Spiritual Intimacy:

> If you have any encouragement from being united with Christ, if any comfort from his love, if any fellowship with the Spirit, if any tenderness and compassion, then make my joy complete by being like-minded, having the same love, being one in spirit and purpose.[22]

1. How encouraging is it to know you are united with Christ? _____
   _____
   _____

2. In ways have you been comforted from the love of Christ and other believers? _____
   _____
   _____

3. What are the benefits of being in fellowship with the Holy Spirit and other spirit-filled believers? _____
   _____
   _____

4. What does it feel like to be received by others with deep affections warmth, tenderness, and compassion? _____
   _____
   _____

So what is the motivation for seeking spiritual intimacy?

Since you are a recipient of encouragement in Christ, comfort, love, tender mercies, and compassion, then it is your obligation to give to your spouse what you have already received. There are tremendous blessings when you and your spouse are relating to one another in a way that reflects the love of Christ.

As stated previously, spiritual intimacy requires having the mind of Christ. The mind of Christ consists of being unified in spirit. It involves humility, sacrifice, obedience, and seeing your spouse as more important than yourself.

22. Philippians 2:1–2 (NIV)

The mind of Christ also means having a biblical worldview. A biblical worldview consists of the following four elements:

An Understanding of God and His Will:

Seeing God for who he is, his greatness, supreme authority, sovereignty, sufficiency, goodness, loving-kindness, and love. It compels you to worship him.

> The heavens are telling of the glory of God; And their expanse is declaring the work of His hands. Day to day pours forth speech, And night to night reveals knowledge.[23]

> For from Him and through Him and to Him are all things. To Him be the glory forever. Amen.[24]

An Understanding of Yourself and God's Will:

Seeing God for who he is compels you and your spouse to have a spirit of humility.

> and My people who are called by My name humble themselves and pray and seek My face and turn from their wicked ways, then I will hear from heaven, will forgive their sin and will heal their land.[25]

An Understanding of Relationships and God's Will:

Seeing God for who he is compels you and your spouse to love God and one another.

> And He said to him, "*You shall love the Lord your God with all your heart, and with all your soul, and with all your mind.*" This is the great and foremost commandment. The second is like it, "*You shall love your neighbor as yourself.*"[26]

23. Psalms 19:1–2 (NASB)
24. Romans 11:36 (NASB
25. 2 Chronicles 7:14 (NASB)
26. Matthew 22:37–39 (NASB)

An Understanding of Unfavorable Circumstances,
Situations, and Events and God's Will:

Seeing God for who he is will promote a biblical response to life's troubles.

> And we know that God causes all things to work together for good to those who love God, to those who are called according to His purpose.[27]

> Consider it all joy, my brethren, when you encounter various trials[28]

> The lord is good, A stronghold in the day of trouble, And He knows those who take refuge in Him.[29]

How can you and your Spouse Achieve Spiritual Intimacy:

- Devotions.
- Bible study.
- Committing to growing in the likeness of Christ.
- Praying for one another.
- Serving together in ministry.
- Worship.

Conclusion:

The purpose of this chapter is to help couples understand, establish, and maintain intimacy through the exercising of oneness in every area of their marriage. The whole objective in your marriage is to reflect the image of God. God created marriage as a covenant of companionship, where both you and your spouse live as one. If you and your spouse commit to applying the principles discussed in the chapter, you will begin to experience physical, emotional, mental, and spiritual intimacy in a way that allows love,

---

27. Romans 8:28 (NASB)
28. James 1:2 (NASB)
29. Nahum 1:7 (NASB)

peace, joy, and harmony to permeate your marriage. The result will be a marriage without misery, one that brings honor and glory to God.

"Reinforce the stitch that ties us, and I will do the same for you."

—DORIS SCHERIN

10

In-Laws and Family Feuds

Counseling Issue:

ASTON AND CHELSEA HAVE been married for two years. There has always been an undertow of frustration and tension between his family and his new wife—Aston struggles to figure out the problem. Aston, the only male child, has a tight-knit family. He and his mother, the family matriarch, are very close. When his mother calls their home, she says a couple of cordial words to Chelsea, then asks that Aston come to the phone. He and his mother frequently talk for well over an hour.

Before marriage, Chelsea assumed Aston's family would accept her into the family circle but now believes his family feels as if she is not "good enough" for him. She feels like an outsider when she is around his family. Chelsea consistently accuses Aston of not standing up for her when his mother makes subtle sarcastic comments to her. Aston believes her unwillingness to accept his family's closeness and tight bond makes her feel left out. Resentment and bitterness continue to build up between Chelsea and Aston's family. He wants his family and his wife to get along. Aston is caught in the middle of a family feud between his family and his wife. He feels like a rope in a tug-of-war. How can he fix the problem?

The Problem:

Chelsea is resentful of Aston's close relationship with his family, particularly his mother. She believes it is Aston's responsibility to fix the issues that his family may have with her. This has caused disunity in the home and marital oneness is difficult to achieve. Chelsea's heart issue is the desire to be accepted and approved of by Aston's family and to be shown love by her husband. Because she is not getting what she desires she has become resentful and bitter toward both her husband and his family. Her bitterness has caused her to withdraw from his family. Whenever she is in a room full of Aston's family, she feels isolated and alone.

Aston has misplaced loyalties and has put his close family bond above oneness with his spouse. Because he is the child and sibling that gets most of the attention in his family, he has a difficult time leaving and cleaving to his wife and becoming one with her. Aston should think less of himself and more of the needs of his wife. Thinking biblically about his marriage can help Aston understand that his wife comes first before his family regardless of how close the family bond is.

Resolving Family Issues:

Some people may say when you marry your spouse, you also marry their family. This statement is not true. You do not marry your in-laws, but you will gain another family—the good, the bad, and the dysfunctional. Your spouse is also a product of that family, and he or she may be predisposed to some habits, hang-ups, and hurts that were taught and passed down through the family. Together, you and your spouse can develop a loving union despite broken, estranged, and dysfunctional family relationships as you grow together to love God, love each other, understand and stand for one another.

As a couple, you can also learn to develop loving relationships with your family and in-laws in a peaceful family unit free of conflict and unforgiveness. It does take time to establish relationships in your new family. You may feel like an outsider at first, but once you have spent enough time getting to know them and how they relate to one another, you will carve your place in the family and in their hearts. You cannot control what happens in the hearts and homes of your extended family, but as for you and your house, you can choose to love like Christ and rid your home and your marriage of generational sin and disunity. If you have in-laws who outwardly and consistently show love and respect to your spouse and your marriage, they will add a welcome source of encouragement and support.

Describe your relationship with your spouse's family: _____

_____

_____

The Bible is clear that the husband must leave his parents and cleave to his wife.

> Therefore, a man shall leave his father and his mother and hold fast to his wife, and they shall become one flesh.[1]

> And said, For this cause shall a man leave father and mother, and shall cleave to his wife: and they twain shall be one flesh.[2]

> For this cause shall a man leave his father and mother, and shall be joined unto his wife, and they two shall be one flesh.[3]

> For this reason, a man will leave his father and mother and be united to his wife[4]

Scripture refers to the sanctity of the marriage relationship when it says, "for this reason." But what is the reason? The reason is that God made woman for man, and the two shall become one flesh! They are to exhibit oneness and unity of spirit and body. The marriage union is created by God to be a mirror reflection of his image: God the father, God the son, and God the Holy Spirit. This means that the relationship of the man with his wife is closer than that to his father and mother.

Why do you believe it is essential for the husband and wife to leave their parent's home in the following ways?

1. Physically: _____

_____

_____

2. Financially: _____

_____

_____

3. Loyalty: _____

_____

_____

1. Genesis 2:24 (NASB)
2. Matthew 19:5–6 (NASB)
3. Ephesians 5:31 (NASB)
4. Mark 10:7 (NASB)

4. Emotionally: _____

_____

_____

Leave Physically:

What potential problems can arise when a married couple moves into their parents' home for an extended time? Your parents' house has its own rules and beliefs, and anyone who lives under their roof should respect them. Your parents have the right to say and do what they choose in their own home—a right you do not have the freedom to exercise in that situation. There cannot be two leaders or two managers of the house. Therefore, the husband must leave the dependency of his parents and cleave to his wife. The wife is also to leave the dependence of her parents and join herself to her husband. Moving out of your parents' home and into your own home helps you and your spouse establish guidelines that govern your own home and your life that are aligned with your beliefs.

What personal freedoms and privacy might you have to give up if you and your spouse were to move in with either of your parent's home; and would your spouse be ok with it? _____

_____

_____

Leave Financially:

A husband and wife must also leave their parents' financial dependence. Sure, situations can arise that may require limited assistance from one's parents, but this should never be the norm. A husband should be able to take care of his wife and provide for his family's needs without the parents' continuous help. As head of the house, the husband is primarily responsible for providing for his own home. Once you have established your own home, make sure you can financially support yourself without the help of your parents. Do not depend on your parents to afford you the standard of living you desire. A husband should provide, with the help of his wife if necessary, a home and lifestyle they can sustain on their own. If a couple cannot establish a home of their own, they should wait until they can support themselves independently without financial help before they decide to marry.

> The lord God took the man and put him in the garden of Eden to work it and keep it.[5]

Genesis 2:15 makes it clear that even the perfection and paradise of the garden was no place for man to be idle and self-indulgent. God assigned him the task of working, tending, preserving, and protecting his resources, which required physical effort and toil.

> For even when we were with you, we would give you this command: If anyone is not willing to work, let him not eat.[6]

Second Thessalonians 3:10 says that any man who will not work should not be afforded the privilege of eating.

> In all toil there is profit, but mere talk tends only to poverty.[7]

If a man can only talk about what he intends to do but never put out any serious effort, it will soon lead to his poverty and want. On the other hand, there are tremendous benefits when a man works to earn wages.

If your parents or in-laws had to support you and your spouse financially on a frequent basis, how do you think that would affect your relationship?

_____

_____

Leave Parental Loyalty:

What would happen if you had to choose between your family or your spouse? Aston, in the counseling situation at the beginning of this chapter, appears to be facing the same dilemma. The fact is, you can have healthy relationships with your family and your spouse's family when you establish that your marriage and your spouse come first. Your family should know that you stand for and with your spouse. This way, no one will be able to create division and strife between you. Your commitment and loyalty to your spouse is not contingent upon whether he or she is right or wrong. The point

5. Genesis 2:15 (ESV)

6. 2 Thessalonians 3:10 (ESV)

7. Proverbs 14:23 (ESV)

is, when you marry, your loyalty belongs to your spouse. Period. If you must choose between your spouse and your family, you have vowed to choose your spouse. He or she must always take first place. Besides your relationship with the Lord, your spouse should be the closest and most important.

Leave Emotionally:

It is not uncommon to have a close emotional bond with your parents or family. Children have a mental and spiritual dependence on their parents to help them through hurts, fears, and to help them manage feelings and emotions. As an adult, you may still depend on parents to help you sort out your feelings and emotions during difficult times. You may even continue, to some extent, to rely on their wisdom, knowledge, and experience when you are facing tough decisions. However, when you are married, you and your spouse will have relational issues and personal problems that should not be shared with your parents. You will have to work through those issues independent of your parents.

Your parents should not become an emotional crutch every time you have marital disagreements or minor or major problems. Sharing too much information with your parents may cause division between your spouse and your family. Even after you and your spouse resolve your issues and move forward, your extended family members may still harbor negative feelings about your spouse, based upon information that you shared. Sometimes that information is shared with other family members as gossip. They may make judgments about your spouse based on your emotional response to the problem. You and your spouse should work out your issues together or seek counsel from a wise, trusted, Christian friend, Biblical Counselor, or Church clergy.

What are some relational issues that can arise when parents become an emotional crutch for your spouse when problems arise in your marriage?

_____

_____

Establish Parental Boundaries and Cleave to your Spouse:

> Honor your father and your mother, as the lord your God com-
> manded you, that your days may be long, and that it may go well
> with you in the land that the lord your God is giving you.[8]

> You know the commandments: 'Do not murder, Do not commit
> adultery, Do not steal, Do not bear false witness, Do not defraud,
> Honor your father and mother.[9]

The Bible commands you to honor your father and mother. The word
"honor" means to esteem and revere. Parents are to be greatly valued and
highly respected. This command is included in the commandments, and
following this will give you a long and prosperous life because of your obedience to the Lord. However, conflict can arise in marriages when parents
or in-laws constantly interject, improperly say and do things, or make judgments about how you manage your household.

Are you experiencing marital conflict because parents or in-laws
intrude in your marriage relationship or expect you to fulfill a need that
goes beyond your responsibility? While the Bible instructs us to honor our
parents, there are parental boundaries that must be set when you marry.
Your parents are not your number one priority. Your spouse becomes your
priority. You are no longer your parents' priority. They should relinquish
that role to your spouse. Parents should respect your marital union and not
interfere in your decisions.

Interference:

> A wise *man* will hear and will increase learning; and a man of un-
> derstanding shall attain unto wise counsel.[10]

Wise counsel from parents and in-laws is excellent, and the Bible says
that a wise person will seek wisdom and knowledge from those who have
walked in their shoes and those who have learned from experience. However, your parents should respect your marriage enough to know when not
to interfere and avoid doing or saying things that cause conflict or division

8. Deuteronomy 5:16 (NASB)
9. Mark 10:19 (NASB)
10. Proverbs 1:5 (NASB)

between you and your spouse. There is a difference between wise counsel and interference. Parents may not always know the difference. Wise counsel imparts biblical truth, godly principles and points you down a path of what is right. Wise counsel will never put you and your spouse at odds with each other but always seeks to offer knowledge and resolution.

What boundaries do you and your spouse need to set as it relates to parents or in-laws? _____

_____

_____

Parents and in-laws may not discern when they are over-reaching or interfering because that may be traditionally how their family has always related to one another. Your spouse may be the one who points out when in-laws are intrusive or meddling. It will be your responsibility to set limits with your family without putting your spouse in the middle. You want your spouse and your family to have a non-contentious relationship with one another. Because of this, in most cases, you should confront the problem with your own family first. If that brings no results, then you and your spouse can respectfully confront them together. If that conversation does not stop the interference, then you and your spouse must set boundaries with your parents or in-laws to assure that your marriage is respected and honored. The goal is to establish a loving, peaceful, and harmonious relationship with your parents and in-laws based on mutual respect and honesty. Remember, your family should know that you stand for and stand with your spouse in agreement and unity.

Role Reversal:

What happens when your spouse's role in his or her family has been reversed, or they have taken on responsibility for providing care for their mother or father? Often spouses may have to take on the responsibility of an elderly, ill, or impoverished parent. The Bible commands us to honor them by taking care of our elderly and widowed parents. Among other things, adult children are to help sustain them when they are reduced to poverty. Read the following verses and write down what each passage has to say about how you are to relate to your parents or the consequences for not caring for them when they are unable to care for themselves:

1. "Listen to your father who gave you life, and do not despise your mother when she is old."[11] _____

_____

_____

2. "But if a widow has children or grandchildren, they must first learn to show godliness to their own family and repay their parents, for this is pleasing in the sight of God."[12] _____

_____

_____

3. "For God commanded, 'Honor your father and your mother,' and, 'Whoever reviles father or mother must surely die.'"[13] _____

_____

_____

4. "Whoever curses his father or mother, his lamp will be extinguished in deepest darkness."[14] _____

_____

_____

5. "But you say that whoever tells his father or mother, 'I have given to God whatever support you might have received from me,' does not have to honor his father. Because of your traditions you have destroyed the authority of God's word."[15] _____

_____

_____

Taking on the care of a parent can be very stressful, especially if you and your spouse are not on one accord. You may or may not receive help and support from other family members in caring for your aging or ill parents. You will need the emotional, physical, and spiritual support of your spouse. Your spouse may need to help fulfill other responsibilities at home. Being a caregiver for your parents or any family member can take a toll on your marriage if you do not have the understanding and support of your spouse. Get help from other relatives, your church family, support groups,

11. Proverbs 23:22 (NASB)
12. 1 Timothy 5:4 (NASB)
13. Matthew 15:4 (NASB)
14. Proverbs 20:20 (NASB)
15. Matthew 15:5–6 (GW)

and family services. Continue to nurture your marriage by taking time out for your spouse to communicate, relax, doing something you enjoy together and for intimacy.

On the other hand, there may be different role reversals that do not fall under God's commands, where boundaries may need to be set. A single or divorced parent who has depended on a son or daughter to fulfill the role of a spouse, not in position but in function, is not uncommon. The son or daughter may have taken on the primary role of a helper, handyman, financial supporter, confidant, or companion. This role reversal may have begun when the child was still in the parents' home and continued well into adulthood. The parent may have a difficult time releasing the adult child and the role he or she has taken on. The parent may still expect them to continue in this role after their son or daughter is married.

If you are experiencing this role reversal, as it relates to a single or divorced parent, you must avoid being manipulated and use good judgment. Understand that your priority is to love and care for your spouse and home. Rightfully, your parents should encourage you to put your spouse first and nurture your marriage relationship. Selfish motives and jealousy will keep parents from doing this. They may even have some animosity toward your spouse because they feel your spouse has taken their place. In this case, you will have to set some boundaries. You should respectfully have a conversation with your parents about how and when you can help. Encourage your mother or father to build relationships with others and find fulfilling activities, social or ministry opportunities to fill any void in their life.

If an adult son or daughter's role has been reversed and the parent remarries, then the adult child may harbor feelings of jealousy, resentment, or fear of being replaced. The parent will have to set some boundaries and communicate with their son or daughter that their spouse holds first place in their life, which is God's will for their marriage. Marriage does not diminish the love toward others but adds fullness as each person in the family relationship takes pleasure in the love and joy that each one brings to one another. This pleases the Lord. It can be a joyful experience when all family members are operating in unison and love.

> then make my joy complete by being of one mind, having the same love, being united in Spirit and purpose.[16]

---

16. Philippians 2:2 (NASB)

1. If you or your spouse are experiencing a role reversal in caring for an elderly, ill or widowed parent, what do you both need to discuss in regard to responsibilities, finances, living arrangements, help from others, and outside resources? _____

   _____

   _____

2. If you or your spouse are experiencing a role reversal because a single or divorced parent is depending on either of you to fulfill the function of a spouse, what agreements need to be discussed and/or boundaries that need to be set? _____

   _____

   _____

Resolving In-law Conflict:

Read the following verses and write down what each passage has to say about how you should respond to being offended or unfairly treated:

1. "A man's insight gives him patience, and his virtue is to overlook an offense."[17] _____

   _____

   _____

2. "For if you forgive men their trespasses, your Heavenly Father will also forgive you."[18] _____

   _____

   _____

3. "Accept one another, then, just as Christ accepted you, in order to bring glory to God."[19] _____

   _____

   _____

17. Proverbs 19:11 (NASB)
18. Matthew 6:14 (NASB)
19. Romans 15:7 (NASB)

4. "with all humility and gentleness, with patience, bearing with one another in love"[20] _____

_____

_____

5. "But I say unto you, Love your enemies, bless them that curse you, do good to them that hate you, and pray for them which despitefully use you, and persecute you"[21] _____

_____

_____

You can have a good and peaceful relationship with your in-laws. Resolving in-law conflict is possible, but it must start with forgiveness. Holding on to unforgiveness and bitterness will only burden you[22] and keep you from experiencing the family unity you desire, even within your own home. Bad relationships with your in-laws affect more than just yourself. When in-law relationships are contentious, estranged, or non-existent, other relationships within both families can become collateral damage. Your children can lose out on joyous, loving, and nurturing relationships with grandparents, or you can impair other relationships within your spouse's family because of disunity and hostility.

Conflict with your in-laws can put your spouse in a very awkward position. Your spouse must choose to stand with and stand for you, yet they still love their family and desire to have a close, loving relationship with them. Your spouse cannot be the go-between in this conflict between you and his or her parents. He or she should encourage you to go to your in-laws and work out the problem between the two of you. Your spouse should also encourage his or her family to resolve conflict with you if they desire to be a part of your family.

A Spouse Can Not Stand Up for Sin:

Although your spouse must stand with you, you cannot expect that they will stand up for sin. If you are wrong, unforgiving, or holding onto bitterness, they must privately hold you accountable as your fellow Christian. If your spouse is wrong or sinning, it is a private matter that is not to be

20. Ephesians 4:2 (NASB)
21. Matthew 5:44 (NASB)
22. Colossians 3:13 (NASB)

discussed with family. The only discussion of sin issues with family should be in the form of personal confession, to seek forgiveness and reconciliation. This accountability includes showing you through the Bible how your actions, behaviors, and attitudes fail to align with God's word in obedience. If you are disobedient to God's word, do not expect your spouse to join you in your disobedience in a united front. You should examine your motives and determine if your course of action is self-serving or pleasing to God.

> Brethren, even if anyone is caught in any trespass, you who are spiritual, restore such a one in a spirit of gentleness; each one looking to yourself, so that you too will not be tempted.[23]

> If your brother sins, go and show him his fault in private; if he listens to you, you have won your brother.[24]

Resolving conflict begins with asking yourself, "What do I want that I am not getting?" Or, "What am I getting that I do not want?" James chapter 4 tells us that the source of conflict is the desires and passions that war within you. When you do not get what you want, you strategize and maneuver as to how you will get it. When you cannot obtain it, you fight and quarrel. You want something from the in-laws you have a conflict with. It may be respect, acceptance, to be viewed as competent, or to be understood. It could be several things. They have within their power to give you these things, but they chose not to. The question is if you are willing to sin to have what you want. If you have ceased all communication, stopped answering your phone, harboring unforgiveness and bitterness, talking badly about them to others, or keeping the children away from them, then you are sinning. Refer to the chapter 7 "The Source of Conflict" and chapter 8 "The Solution for Conflict."

> What causes quarrels and what causes fights among you? Is it not this, that your passion are at war within you? You desire and do not have, so you murder. You covet and cannot obtain, so you fight and quarrel. You do not have, because you do not ask. You ask and do not receive, because you ask wrongly, to spend it on your passions.[25]

23. Galatians 6:1 (NASB)
24. Matthew 18:15 (NASB)
25. James 4:1–3 (NASB)

Conclusion:

So, what do you do when you are experiencing conflict with in-laws? You must stand in one accord with your spouse and allow nothing and no one to cause division and chaos in your marital relationship. Do what you are responsible for doing. If it is a personal conflict between you and your in-laws, do not rely on your spouse to make it right. Plan a proper time and place to have a conversation with the person you have conflict. Acknowledge that conflict between the two of you is not what you desire. Start with asking for forgiveness for anything you have said or done to offend them. If you have hurt them, take responsibility for it. Even if you do not know or remember the offense, ask questions for clarity and understanding. Do not say, "If you think I offended you . . ." You must acknowledge there has been an offense, intentional or unintentional, and ask for forgiveness.

Let them know that you desire a peaceful, loving relationship with them, and you wish to harbor no hostility or hard feelings. Tell them if they are willing, you want a fresh start to building a relationship based on mutual love and respect. If they are not receptive, leave the door open for reconciliation. Pray for them and ask God to soften their hearts and bring restoration to your relationship. Continue to show love toward them and try to keep the peace. You may ask: "But why should I do this?" or "Why should I make the effort when my in-Laws seem more like my enemies?"

Your efforts and obedience will please the Lord and keep you from the guilt of the unforgiveness (which is sin) and the misery of a family divided. Meditate on the following Scriptures. Write down at least two things you can do to apply each of them to your life:

1. "For this *finds* favor, if for the sake of conscience toward God a person bears up under sorrows when suffering unjustly. For what credit is there if, when you sin and are harshly treated, you endure it with patience? But if when you do what is right and suffer *for it* you patiently endure it, this *finds* favor with God."[26] _____

_____

_____

---

26. 1 Peter 2:19–20 (NASB)

2. "When a man's ways please the lord, he makes even his enemies to be at peace with him."[27] _____

_____

_____

3. "If possible, so far as it depends on you, be at peace with all men."[28] __

_____

_____

4. "Do not be overcome by evil, but overcome evil with good."[29] _____

_____

_____

27. Proverbs 16:7 (NASB)
28. Romans 12:18 (NASB)
29. Romans 12:21 (NASB)

11

Blended Families are Real Families

Counseling Issue:

THOMAS AND KELLIE ARE a newly-married couple in their late thirties. They are both divorcees and have children from previous marriages. Thomas is very close to his daughter, Shana, and spends as much time as possible with her—well beyond the visitation agreement in the divorce settlement. Kellie has a son, Jonathan, from her first marriage, who has a great relationship with his biological father. The children often engage in arguments with one another as each compete to get attention. Kellie is a bit jealous of the extra time Thomas gives his daughter and desires to spend more time with her new husband. Thomas feels as if Kellie is hesitant to embrace Shana as her daughter. He believes Kellie should take more time to build a closer relationship with her. Kellie's ex-husband is concerned about his son and what influences Thomas will have on his very impressionable child while living with Thomas and his ex-wife, Kellie, the custodial parent. Tensions are building between Kellie's ex-husband, Thomas, Kellie, and among the children.

The Problem:

Thomas and Kellie are not functioning as a family. There appears to be a great divide between the parents, the ex-spouse, and between the children. They are experiencing contentions, hostility, and chaos in the home. Every family member is always on edge, irritable, or angry about something. This blended family is suffering in disfunction and distress. Is there any hope for a blended family in this condition? Absolutely!

Objective:

The purpose of this chapter is to help couples avoid the misery of disfunction in blended families, to lead and guide blended families to live together in unconditional love, and to help couples learn how to function, not just as a blended family, but as a real family.

If you have children by another marriage or have been a part of a blended family, then you know that blended families can bring challenges, especially to new a marriage—children, ex-spouses, biological parents, extended families, and traditions can all create additional problems. Nevertheless, you and your spouse need to know how to navigate these issues biblically. Prayerfully, if you commit to using God's word as your guide, you can have a blended family that is saturated with love, respect, and acceptance. Remember, you and your spouse must bring your home in order under God's authority. All other people and situations that affect your home fall under the same protective and sovereign authority.

Building Blended Family Relationships:

Stepfamilies and blended families are created when a husband and wife marry and one or both have children from a previous marriage or relationship. The acceptance of a new wife or husband in the parent's life can sometimes be difficult for biological children. Building relationships in blended families can sometimes be complicated for the husband, the wife, the exes, and the extended family. Just like in-laws, children and stepchildren need to understand that the husband and wife have a united front. They stand for and stand with one another. Most importantly, they need to understand that your marital union is established and guided by God's word.

Guidelines to Becoming a Real Family:

Establish a Godly Foundation:

Your goal as a family is to establish and maintain a godly, Christian home. A home where Christ is the head and authority. A home where God is worshipped, and his word is the guiding principle. Your home should be a place where the love for God and one another is the abiding factor that holds everything together. You and your spouse's words, actions, and attitudes toward one another, the children, and extended family will be evidence that this guiding principle is instituted in the home.

Building and Rebuilding Trusting Relationships:

If you are a part of a blended family, then there has been a loss or dissolution of another family unit. There may have been a covenant (sexual) relationship that did not result in a marriage union. For your blended family to function as its best with every family member experiencing good emotional and spiritual health, you must do the work of building new relationships and the rebuilding of damaged relationships.

Building trusting relationships with your stepchildren will take time and patience. Children will need time to know the new parent and the stepparent must understand how to communicate with them properly. It is easy for most children to understand and pick up cues from their parents, through both verbal and non-verbal communication. A child can discern from a parent's facial expressions and body language what the parent is communicating. A "think twice" look from a parent communicates limitations without being frightening. However, from a stepparent, that same facial expression or body language might seem intimidating or hostile.

The longer your stepchildren spend time getting to know you, the easier it will be to gain acceptance as their parent's new spouse. When parents divorce, the child or children often become the most important person in the life of a single parent. When a parent remarries, their new spouse now becomes the number one person in their life. This shift in prioritized relationships will sometimes provoke a child to compete for the biological parent's attention. Even when a child feels loved and secure, it does not always mean that a new spouse will not make the child feel threatened by this relationship.

A child may attempt to test the loyalty of their parent by testing if the parent will put him or her first, believe them, or take their side over their spouse. The biological parent may feel as if they are in a tug of war between the child and the spouse. A test of loyalties is a test of who you will be faithful to. As a parent, you must remain faithful to God and obedient to his word. Continue to hold the child to God's standards. Continue to choose a child's obedience over a child's pleasure. Continue to respond to the child according to what is right. Do not respond out of your feelings of guilt over a previous divorce or the fact that you have a new spouse who now takes first place over your child.

The Bible tells us to put on "compassionate hearts."[1] Pray to the Lord to help soften your heart toward your stepchild(ren) even when they are hard to love. Show them by example that you have chosen to love, to be kind and gentle. This way, after they understand that you are not going to compete with them, get angry, irritated, or battle for their respect, they will eventually let their guard down. As they experience the loving, godly, and genuine person you are, they will also come to realize that a relationship with you is not a threat but a value. Be ready to forgive the offenses of your stepchildren and remain patient, bearing with their feelings of jealousy, avoidance, and their unwillingness to receive your efforts to love and build a close relationship.

> Put on then, as God's chosen ones, holy and beloved, compassion-
> ate hearts, kindness, humility, meekness, and patience, bearing with
> one another and, if one has a complaint against another, forgiving
> each other; as the Lord has forgiven you, so you also must forgive[2]

Biological and stepparents should also be aware that children might attempt to manipulate them to get what they want or may attempt to cause division in their marriage. Children can discern when parents are not in one accord or not effectively communicating and use that to their advantage. If one parent says no, they may ask the other. They might try even harder with the stepparent, hoping they will give-in easily to gain the child's acceptance. You must make decisions with your spouse privately and be in one accord so that the children know and understand they cannot use one parent against the other or use your discord to drive a wedge between the two of you.

Additionally, a divorced parent may need to rebuild trust with their child if that child has witnessed a bitter and continuous relationship between the biological parents. Building trust is also necessary after a divorce where the child was caught in the middle of the battle. The child needs to understand that the divorce is not their fault. Explain to them that although the marriage could not be healed, your relationship, bond, support,

1. Colossians 3:12–14 (ESV)
2. Colossians 3:12–14 (ESV)

and most importantly, love for them, will never change and will never be separated or terminated. Encourage the child or children that they are not a burden or nuisance, but a significant part of your life, your new marriage, and home.

Giving Hope After the Loss of a Parent:

If a biological parent has died before the new marriage, a child will need time to accept the new spouse in their parent's life. Unlike divorce, where a choice was made to dissolve the marriage, the death of a parent is not chosen or desired. The loss of a spouse or a parent leaves a void that no person can replace. Talk with your spouse about how your child has dealt with the loss. When a parent remarries after the death of a spouse, the child may experience feelings of grief and act-out. They may refuse to accept and embrace the new spouse's attempt to show love and affection toward them.

In some cases, widows and widowers may allow indulgences, withhold discipline, or fail to establish a structure to compensate for the loss that the child(ren) has experienced. Parents should be aware that boundaries, training, and structure all help the child deal with life's challenges in a way that builds character, endurance and hope.[3] Encourage the child that their mom or dad could never be replaced, because they hold a unique place in your life and heart.

Children may also show bitterness toward their biological parent for moving forward in life with a new spouse. They may interpret this to mean that their living parent has forgotten about their deceased spouse and have abandoned the memories of the family unit. The biological parent can make sure the child has grieved and has learned how to express their grief in a God-pleasing way. A member of the clergy or a counselor can help the child deal with their grief and walk them through the healing process.

Whether being a single parent is a result of a divorce or the death of a spouse, talk to your child(ren) about God's ability to help them through their fears, hurts, sadness, and loneliness. Help your child understand that God loves them and cares about what they are going through. Read the following scriptures and write down what each says about God's ability to help, to heal, and teach them to your children:

3. Romans 5:3–5 (NASB)

1. "The lord is near to the brokenhearted And saves those who are crushed in spirit."[4] _____

   _____

   _____

2. "Blessed are those who mourn, for they shall be comforted."[5] _____

   _____

   _____

3. "He heals the brokenhearted And binds up their wounds."[6] _____

   _____

   _____

4. "Blessed *be* the God and Father of our Lord Jesus Christ, the Father of mercies and God of all comfort, who comforts us in all our affliction so that we will be able to comfort those who are in any affliction with the comfort with which we ourselves are comforted by God."[7] _____

   _____

   _____

5. "casting all your anxiety on Him, because He cares for you."[8] _____

   _____

   _____

Pray the above verses with your children and remind them that God is near to the brokenhearted.[9] He bandages our wounds and does a work of healing in our lives.[10] The same comfort and healing God provided the grieving spouse, he can give to the children through their parent.[11] The husband and wife should talk about how they have dealt with the loss and decide if counseling is needed. You must continue to build trusting relationships with your stepchildren by assuring them of your love for them and your genuine concern for what they are going through.

4. Psalms 34:18 (NASB)

5. Matthew 5:4 (NASB)

6. Psalms 147:3 (NASB)

7. 2 Corinthians 1:3–4 (NASB)

8. 1 Peter 5:7 (NASB)

9. Psalms 34:18; Matthew 5:4 (NASB)

10. Psalms 147:3 (NASB)

11. 2 Corinthians 1:3–4 (NASB)

Make Sure That the Parent–Child Relationship Is in Its Rightful Place:

While the parent-child relationship should be one of unconditional love, provision, and protection—the union of husband and wife is sacred, and it comes first. It is a "one flesh" covenant relationship. After God created Eve for Adam, the Book of Genesis says, "For this reason a man will leave his father and mother and be united to his wife, and they will become one flesh."[12] It is more acceptable today for a husband and wife to leave or abandon one another than it is for a parent to leave or forsake a child. But God intended marriage to last a lifetime. The marriage relationship should be the number one earthly relationship we have.

The Bible says that God hates divorce.[13] The Bible also shows that adultery is the only permissible reason for divorce.[14] Since God views a sexual union as a covenantal act of marriage,[15] the covenant of marriage is broken when a husband or wife commits adultery. God forgives and can bless remarriage after divorce for those with a contrite and repentant heart.[16] Because of the high rate of divorce and brevity of marriage—even among Christians—we often prioritize our relationship with our children over our spouse.

Because marriage is a sacred covenant, the parent–child relationship should be third, after your relationship with God and your spouse. Children and stepchildren should understand their place in the family, not as it relates to love and acceptance, but as it relates to position. They must be taught and understand that your new marriage is established by God, honored by God's promises, and built on a foundation of God's word. Spouses must understand this as well and avoid placing the parent–child relationship over their marriage.

Leadership in the home needs to be established:

Because there has been only one parent in your home or your spouse's home, leadership needs to be established with the children and young

12. Genesis 2:24 (NASB)
13. Malachi 2:16 (NASB)
14. Matthew 19:3–9; Mark 10:11–12 (NASB)
15. Genesis 20:23–25, 24:67; Deuteronomy 21:10 (NASB)
16. Acts 3:19; Ephesians 1:7–8; Psalms 103:10–12 (NASB)

adults. The Bible is clear that the husband is the head of the household. Read the following scriptures and write down what each says about leadership in the home:

1. "He must manage his own household well, with all dignity keeping his children submissive."[17] _____

   _____

   _____

2. "But I want you to understand that the head of every man is Christ, the head of a wife is her husband, and the head of Christ is God."[18] __

   _____

   _____

3. "For if someone does not know how to manage his own household, how will he care for God's church?"[19] _____

   _____

   _____

4. "Wives, submit to your husbands, as is fitting in the Lord."[20] _____

   _____

   _____

Fathers are to be the primary leaders in the home. However, fathers and mothers are the authority over the children. Parents who have been single for an extended period of time may have children of a certain age that have experienced a role reversal. A son might fill the role of the husband and father because of the absence of a man in the home. He may be doing certain chores and physical tasks; he may also feel responsible for protecting both his mother and his younger siblings. He has a heightened awareness of strangers and situations out of the ordinary. A daughter of a certain age might fill the role of the wife and mother in the home. She may have become the organizer, household manager, prepare meals for the family, and help the father keep the house and younger siblings in order.

These roles will now be managed by the stepfather or stepmother or delegated to others. Encourage the child that their part in the family unit is essential. Gently and lovingly step into parental roles as necessary and

17. 1 Timothy 3:4 (ESV)
18. 1 Corinthians 11:3 (ESV)
19. 1 Timothy 3:5 (ESV)
20. Colossians 3:18 (ESV)

let the child release these responsibilities. One of the parent's purposes is to help the children reach their full potential without the burden of taking on adult responsibilities when there is an adult in the parental role. The child's responsibilities should be under the management and guidance of the parents and the head of the home.

Some mothers may have been single for a long time before getting married. During this time, she has been the sole authority and leader in the home. Now that she is married, it may be a struggle for her to hand over her leadership and authority to her new husband. Although it will not come easy, a wife who was a single mother must relinquish her role as head of the home. When a wife fails to align herself with her biblical role and fails to respect the husband's position, the children will also fail to give the husband respect. When children and stepchildren see the wife honoring the husband's position and giving the lead to her husband, headship in the home is established and accepted. The children also need to see the husband stepping into his leadership role with godly, loving, patient, and sacrificial authority. The children should see examples of the husband loving his wife and putting her first, before his own needs.[21] Leadership is sacrificial, and there is no better way to teach this biblical principle than when you love like Christ. Nevertheless, leadership in a Christian home should align with Scripture.

The responsibility to give unconditional love, provision, and protection to your children will now be a joint responsibility of you and your spouse. Where children are involved, there should be no time limit as to how long it takes you to get to know and understand your spouse *before* you marry him or her, when you are giving them this significant responsibility.

1. What are some of the adult responsibilities that your children or stepchildren have taken on that can now be managed, delegated, or taken over by a new parent? _____

   _____

   _____

2. How have you, your spouse, children, or stepchildren responded to authority in your home? _____

   _____

   _____

21. Philippians 2:3 (NASB)

Establishing House Rules and a Code of Conduct:

Every home need rules, guidelines, and a code of conduct. This is especially important when there is a new stepparent or new stepchildren in the home. You and your spouse need to talk about the current rules, what is not being adhered to, and what is not being monitored. You may need to make new rules and set boundaries to establish areas of privacy and acceptable behaviors as you are seeking to live together as one harmonized family unit. You and your spouse will need to discuss the distribution of chores and responsibilities for the children and young adults. Curfews and acceptable language should be established. If children are moving into a different house with the new spouse, then the rules and expectations should be established as soon as possible.

Expectations Need to be Established:

Biological children and stepchildren should know what their parents expect of them when it comes to behavior inside and outside of the home. Respect, truthfulness, and godly behavior are paramount. Some expectations of parents may include church attendance, school attendance, passing grades, friends, activities, mealtimes, and bedtimes. Problems will arise when the child is allowed certain privileges and liberties in the ex-spouse's home that are prohibited in your own. You cannot control what goes on in the other parent's home, but you and your spouse can establish specific standards to be followed in your home and be clear that they are non-negotiable.

You can also equip the child with God's word on how to deal with temptation and corrupt company.[22] If the child is a believer, the Holy Spirit can and will guide the child to flee ungodly and dangerous situations. The child will adjust to the consistent standards you put in place with the hope that your prayers and example of godly living and obedience will prevail over any ungodly behavior they are allowed or exposed to outside of your home. The promise of Proverbs 20:7 encourages us to live by example: "The righteous who walks in his integrity—blessed are his children after him!" But keep in mind that the Bible also says that foolishness is bound up in the heart of a child.[23] So do not expect your child to think and behave like an adult or make decisions as you would. They may not always adhere to the

22. 1 Corinthians 15:22; Proverbs 22:25; Galatians 6:7; James 1:14 (NASB)
23. Proverbs 22:15 (NASB)

godly standards you teach them or heed the guidance of the Holy Spirit. Nevertheless, you must give them grace when they make errors, let them learn from their mistakes through discipline and consequences that allow them to be wiser and stronger from the experience. Extend the same grace God has extended to you.

Appropriate Methods of Discipline Need to be Established:

Along with rules and guidelines, you will also have to discuss methods of discipline and the consequences of not adhering to the rules and expectations. The expectations that you both have of your children, in terms of their behavior, respectful communication, responsibilities, and overall contribution to the household, must be specific, clearly communicated, and understood by your children. The method of discipline should also be discussed, which should be godly discipline, administered in love, not anger, and be appropriate for the age of the child and the offense. Parents must also remember that grace shown toward a child can also be suitable for minor offenses.

Contrary to the word of God, some may believe that a stepparent should not discipline their stepchildren. There may also be circumstances where the other biological parent objects to the stepparent disciplining their child. This can be problematic in the relationship between you, your spouse, and the biological parent. Both biological parents can discuss the method of discipline. However, the *godly discipline* you administer in your own home should not be interfered with or determined by anyone outside of your home.

> Discipline your children, for in that there is hope; do not be a willing party to their death.[24]

> The rod and reproof give wisdom, but a child left to himself brings shame to his mother.[25]

The ex-spouse may not agree with your methods of discipline, but your decision to administer godly discipline is the responsibility of you and your new spouse. If either biological parent believes the stepparent should not discipline the child, that sends the wrong message about the stepparent's authority over the child and the obedience and respect that the child must

24. Proverbs 19:18 (NASB)
25. Proverbs 29:15 (NASB)

give the stepparent. If the stepfather is forbidden to discipline the stepchild, that also sends the wrong message about who is the authority in the home.

Furthermore, the husband does not always have to be the disciplinarian, but as head of the home, he does need to authorize it with his stamp of approval. Discipline for both the biological and stepchildren should be age-appropriate, consistent, and without partiality. Guide the heart of the child when dealing with sin and disobedience. Deal with the sin issue at the heart of the behavior. Deal with the anger, envy, jealousy, or fear and how it has manifested in the wrong response or attitude (as will be discussed in chapter 13).

The goal of all discipline is helping your children live to glorify God. To do so, the child or young adult must acknowledge their wrongdoing as disobedience to God and the parents (confession), and a change in behavior and attitude (repentance) is required. When this goal is accomplished, be ready to forgive and restore the child to the loving parent–child fellowship you had before the offense and do not bring up his or her wrongdoing as a reminder of their imperfections. Bringing up past mistakes is an indication of unforgiveness.

Psalms 103:8–13 paints a beautiful portrait of how our heavenly father disciplines us. Parents in blended families are God-ordained authorities. Read the following verses, consider God's methods of discipline, and write down actions, attitudes, and behaviors that loving parents should exhibit when disciplining their children:

1. "The lord *is merciful and gracious,* slow to anger and abounding in steadfast love."[26] _____
   _____
   _____

2. "He will not always chide [express disapproval or scold], nor will he keep his anger forever."[27] _____
   _____
   _____

26. Psalms 103:8 (NASB)

27. Psalms 103:9 (NASB)

3. "He does not deal with us according to our sins, nor repay us according to our iniquities."[28] _____

_____

_____

4. "For as high as the heavens are above the earth, so great is his steadfast love toward those who fear him"[29] _____

_____

_____

5. "as far as the east is from the west, so far does he remove our transgressions from us."[30] _____

_____

_____

6. "As a father shows compassion to his children, so the lord *shows compassion to those who fear him.*"[31] _____

_____

_____

Consistency and Understanding in Shared Custody and Visitation:

There may already be an agreement of visitation or shared custody of the children in place. If this agreement is working for the biological parents, then the new stepparent should be aware of it, and this arrangement should be worked into the family schedule and weekly routine. If possible, try not to alter the child's schedule or routine in visiting with their other parent. There will already be enough changes in the child's life as they adjust to a new stepparent, stepfamily, or new environment. Sometimes, the biological parents may have flexibility they are willing to extend to each other when it comes to visitation, transportation, or activities for the children. Stepparents should also be willing to be flexible. The adults should have good communication, transparency, and an understanding that there may be certain times that plans and obligations prevent them from being flexible or changing the visitation schedule. Anger, disagreements, and conflict can

28. Psalms 103:10 (NASB)
29. Psalms 103:11 (NASB)
30. Psalms 103:12 (NASB)
31. Psalms 103:13 (NASB)

be avoided when parents and stepparents communicate and work together. As co-parents, the adults should always be ready to extend grace to one another and keep the physical, emotional, and spiritual well-being of the child in view.

Lastly, do not make the mistake of blaming, criticizing, or punishing your spouse for the inconsistencies and failures of his or her ex-spouse to comply with the shared custody and visitation agreement. Respectfully share your concerns with your spouse and allow him or her the opportunity to address the issues with their ex-spouse. If this does not remedy the problem, then both of you may want to discuss the concern with the ex-spouse together, or you can have an adult-to-adult conversation with the ex-spouse. If the ex-spouse is unwilling to compromise or make corrections, then you must set boundaries. Nonetheless, you must make every effort to keep the peace in your relations with the other person.

Avoid Idolizing your Child:

Children are a blessing and a heritage from the Lord.[32] A parent should pour all their efforts into rearing a healthy, confident, and emotionally-balanced child who has been trained in the discipline and instruction of the Lord.[33] Yet a child should not become an idol. Parents should be mindful that when a child is the absolute center of their world and no one else—not even the spouse or the Lord—can instruct, advise, or give constructive criticism about your child, then the child has become an idol. An idol is anything or anyone that takes the place of God and sits on the throne of your heart.

You can know if your child is an idol if you are under the delusion that your child can do no wrong. If you allow your child to exercise authority over you, you have idolized your child. If you believe you are obligated to sacrifice everything for your child to make them happy, then you are guilty of idolatry. If you are willing to sin (lie, steal, manipulate, or scheme), then you are guilty. If you put your child before your spouse or refuse to give your spouse authority over your biological child, then that is sin. If you withhold discipline and allow your child to be disrespectful and disobedient to you or your spouse, then your child is also in sin alongside you.

---

32. Psalms 127:3 (NASB)
33. Ephesians 6:4 (NASB)

Hold your child accountable to God-ordained authority—this means you and your spouse, their teachers, pastor, and governmental authorities. Establish the correct parent–child relationship; set boundaries for your children, and do not parent out of your emotions. Set limits and do not let the child make your decisions and manage your time. Most importantly, teach them God's word so they may come to a saving knowledge and love of God, and submit to God's ultimate authority over their lives.

> Do not turn to idols or make for yourselves molten gods; I am the lord your God.[34]

"Parents who idolize their children are unable to say the word, 'No!'"

—ANONYMOUS

Conclusion:

Applying the principles in this chapter will help you and the members of your new family to function, not just as a blended family, but as a real family. As you know, blended families can bring challenges to a marriage, especially new a marriage. Nevertheless, you and your spouse must navigate through these multitude of problems and difficulties, biblically. If you apply God's word to your marriage and family, and allow his word to guide you, you will have a family that is saturated with love, respect, and acceptance. Keep in mind that you and your spouse must bring your home in order under God's authority. All other people and situations that affect your home fall under the same protective and sovereign authority.

Your goal is to establish and maintain a godly home, a place where God is worshipped and the love for God and one another is the abiding factor that holds everything together. How can this be accomplished? How can a blended family genuinely function as a real family that worships the Lord?

---

34. Leviticus 19:4 (NASB)

You Can Have a Loving, Emotionally- and Spiritually-healthy Blended Family that is a Real Family by:

- Building and rebuilding trusting relationships.
- Making sure that the parent–child relationship is in its rightful place.
- Establishing leadership in the home.
- Establishing house rules and a code of conduct.
- Specifying and communicating your expectations to your children.
- Exercising appropriate methods of discipline.
- Consistency and understanding in shared custody and visitation.
- Avoid idolizing your child.

"Family isn't always blood. It is the people in your life who want you in theirs, the ones who accept you for who you are. The ones that would do anything to see you smile and who love you no matter what. Family is not defined by our genes; it is built and maintained through love."

—ANONYMOUS

12

The Ultimate Marriage Stressor
Money, Debt, and Finances

Counseling Issue:

TREY AND DEB HAVE been married for only a few months. Trey noticed that Deb had a strange habit of being in a hurry to get the mail from the mailbox. She usually was the first to arrive home from work, but one day Deb had to work late, so Trey took the liberty to retrieve the mail from the mailbox. Nestled in-between the usual junk mail, he saw what looked like a credit card statement that was addressed to Deb with the words, "please open immediately," stamped on the front. So he opened it and was floored by what he saw. It was a letter from a collection agency demanding payment for twelve-thousand dollars on a delinquent credit card account. When Deb arrived home, Trey was waiting for her in rage. Trey and Deb engaged in a fiery argument. Trey demanded to know precisely how much debt Deb owed. Deb finally disclosed that she had thirty-five thousand dollars in delinquent credit card bills. Not long after this incident, Trey and Deb decided to get a divorce.

Larry was just twenty-one years old when he married Jae, his high school sweetheart. Larry always felt that a real man's responsibility is to provide for his wife. Jae worked part-time, but Larry was insistent on paying most of the bills without her help. They bought their first starter home after six months of being married. One day, while Larry was at work, Jae signed for a certified letter from the bank that was hand-delivered to the house. She opened it and found that the bank had started foreclosure proceedings on their home because they had not received mortgage payments in two consecutive months. Jae immediately called Larry at work, demanding an explanation. Larry honestly admitted that he got so far behind on the payments that he could not seem to catch up, and he was too prideful to ask for help. Larry ended up working two jobs for six months. The good news is they were able to save their home, but it put a tremendous strain on their marriage. Larry and Jae hardly spoke to one another and refrained from having sex for six months.

Bobby and Mary have been married for three years. Bobby is a blue-collar worker earning good wages. Mary has a professional career where she makes over six figures. Mary earns almost twice as much as Bobby. Bobby and Mary have been experiencing constant conflict throughout their marriage. Bobby complains that Mary spends way too much money. He says that it is not unusual for Mary to return home with bags loaded with merchandise—Louis Vuitton and Gucci products are her favorite. Mary refers to Bobby as being cheap. Mary also feels that she should have the freedom to buy whatever she wants whenever she wants it, regardless of the price. Besides, she says, it's her money, and she can do whatever she wants with it. Mary plans big vacations for both of them and believes it should not be a problem for Bobby since she is paying for it. Bobby feels inadequate as a husband. He believes that Mary is trying to exercise authority over him because she earns more than he does. Bobby and Mary have heated arguments over money regularly.

The Problem:

The common thread in all three of these situations is conflict over finances. Money, if misused, can become an object of devotion and worship. The love of money has separated families and shatter friendships. When money becomes more important than people, any threat or opposition to one's relationship with his money will be met with hostility. Countless marriages have split up over the love of, or the misuse of finances. More couples fight over money, debt, and financial management than any other issue.

Financial difficulties can drive people to depression, loss of appetite, insomnia, and substance abuse. Debt that exceeds one's income can put tremendous pressure on the husband and wife's relationship. Sometimes, a husband and wife will allow the pressure to build up and then unleash the load, the anger, and worry on one another. They take their frustration out on one another when they should be standing together to tackle the internal, external, and sometimes unavoidable, money issues head-on.

Questions to Ponder:

- Do you ever find yourself worrying about how you are going to make ends meet?
- Are you having difficulty sleeping at night due to financial stress?
- Do you and your spouse often argue about finances?
- Do you or your spouse consider your individual earnings to be your money alone?
- Have you lost your desire to be intimate with your spouse because of your financial situation?
- Do you or your spouse refer to a desire as a need?
- Do you put your job before your family?
- How often do you compare yourself with others regarding material possessions, financial freedom, vacations, and wealth?
- What would you do if you lost everything you had; would you consider your life as being over?

If your answer is yes to any of the questions, then there's a word of encouragement for you in this chapter.

Purpose:

The purpose of this chapter is to lay bare biblical truths as it relates to money and to help husbands and wives obtain a biblical perspective about their monetary resources in a way that establishes oneness and brings honor and glory to God. The goal is to equip and encourage married couples to establish and maintain oneness during differing views of money and finances and to avoid the unnecessary difficulties and misery that often occurs as a result of mismanagement—an unrealistic and unbiblical view of money.

The World's View Regarding Money:

For decades, the maxim, "live the American Dream," was the pursuit of many Americans. The American Dream is the belief that anyone, regardless of where they were born or what economic class they come from, has the freedom and the right to pursue happiness through economic success. The focus is on materialism and the right to acquire wealth.

Now we live in a world of classism. The stereotypes, beliefs, and values that one attributes to certain people based upon their character, ability, worth and social class is considered classism. Classism occurs when the under-educated, blue-collar workers are viewed as inferior to the middle-class and middle management. It also occurs when the middle-class are viewed as inferior to the higher-educated upper-class. A person who believes he is superior to the poor, disadvantaged, and those that earn less or who do not have advanced degrees is a classist. In most cases, the amount of wealth one possesses is the measuring rod for self-worth and the catalyst for acceptance into certain upper-class social groups.

So, what are some of the most popular worldviews and beliefs about money and wealth? Here are a few:

- More money means more happiness.
- Money is the answer to most, if not all, of my problems.
- Money sets me apart from others who are less fortunate.
- More money earns me more respect from others.
- Money gives me the freedom to do whatever I chose to do whenever I want.
- Money makes me powerful.
- Money will deliver me from punishment when I have broken the law.
- Money gives me acceptance.
- Money will help me to live longer.
- Money is my security and protector.
- Money gives me value and worth.
- Money is my savior and my lord.
- Money always leaves me wanting more of it.

What is wrong with the world's view regarding money? The world idolizes money. The world worships and has a love of money. Idolatry is to worship something else in place of God. Money is idolized when people believe it is a savior, deliverer, protector, the key to happiness, and the measure of success. Wealth may be viewed as the end all be all. An idol is a person, place, or thing that one runs to for comfort, significance, fulfillment, personal gratification, and to find meaning in life. The object you idolize is the thing that takes place as a master in your life. Your master is who or what you serve and obey. The Master rules.

The Bible's View Regarding Money:

The Bible has a lot to say about money. Just consider the following statistics:

- There are more than two thousand Scriptures on tithing, money, and possessions in the Bible, which is twice as many as faith and prayer combined.

- Sixteen out of thirty-eight of Jesus's parables deal with money and possessions.

- Nearly 25 percent of Jesus's words in the New Testament deal with stewardship.

- One out of ten verses in the Gospels deal with money.[1]

The word of God is replete with instructions on how to handle wealth. It provides guidelines for just about everything related to money and possessions, including budgeting, financial crisis, greed, giving to the poor, investing, lending, retirement, paying taxes, savings, and employment—the list goes on.

Contrary to the world's view of money, Jesus says: "No one can serve two masters; for either he will hate the one and love the other, or he will be devoted to one and despise the other. You cannot serve God and wealth."[2]

Jesus's statement in Matthew 6:24 says that we may be inclined toward one against the other. It is not the possession of money that's at issue, but the serving of it. Jesus says in the first part of this text that no one can serve two masters and bookends the passage by reiterating what he said at the beginning. Jesus also identifies the two masters. In the middle of the

1. Preaching Today, "Statistic: Jesus' Teachings on Money," lines 2–3.
2. Matthew 6:24 (NASB)

bookends, Jesus gives us all the reasons why serving both is impossible. He provides four responses to God and wealth.

The problem is no one can serve two masters. No one means not one single person is capable of serving God and wealth at the same time. Ultimately, it is an impossible task for anyone to accomplish.

What does it mean to "serve?" To serve means involuntary submission to one who is superior. It is something you do out of obligation and is not necessarily based on feelings. Jesus says you will hate one and love the other. You will hate God and love wealth, or you will hate wealth and love God. That is, you will either detest and intensely dislike one and lovingly serve the other out of duty, respect, and reverence with faithfulness. Not one can straddle the fence.

Then Jesus goes on to say, you will be devoted to one and despise the other. You will either be devoted to God and despise wealth, or you will be dedicated to wealth and hate God. In other words, you will either hold firmly to, cleave to, cling to one, or have a distaste for, hold in contempt, think lightly of, neglect, or not care much at all for the other. There is no middle of the road or compromise between serving God and wealth. You are either on one side of the road or the other.

"When it comes to money, we will either worship wealth or worship with our wealth. Money itself may be amoral. But it is our attachment to and our worship of money that will lead us into sin and making poor financial decisions."

—JESSE WISNEWSKI

So how can a husband and wife establish and maintain oneness during financial difficulties so that they will be able to avoid the unnecessary misery and conflict that often occurs because of unrealistic views and mismanagement of money?

You Must View Money and Finances in Terms of Oneness not Individualism:

One of the most common areas couples practice individualism is in finances. In chapter 4, Differences, Expectations and Preferences, we discussed individualism and the spouse who wants to live independently of their mate. They want to make their own decisions and have their own preferences without ever compromising. This is a person whose only concern is self. This is true especially with money and finances. Problems arise when a spouse attempts to stand alone in self-sufficiency within their marriage. They see things in terms of me and mine, and you and yours.

A spouse who practices individualism with money and finances see their income, savings, and investments as theirs alone. It is untouchable and non-negotiable. In chapter 7, Conflict, we discussed the occasions and inducement for conflict. When money and investments are kept outside of the marriage union, it is also outside of God's will for your marriage. A spouse who practices this is saying that, "My money and investments are outside of my spouse's jurisdiction and they have no rights to them." This includes "my bank account," "my car," "my mail," etc." This spouse is only willing to invest a limited amount of what they have in the marriage union.

A couple can never experience oneness when this kind of individualism is practiced. Total control over anything that you deny your spouse access to is an attempt to control your spouse. Some spouses might believe that whatever they maintain control over, they can protect themselves from uncertainty, misuse, mismanagement, or a failed marriage. It is also an attempt to maintain self-sufficiency. This kind of thinking can set your marriage up for failure. This contingency plan will become your hope and what you trust in instead of God and keep you from fighting for your marriage in troubled times. God can do much more through your faith and obedience than you could ever do alone.

When money and finances are viewed in terms of oneness in marriage then it is never "I and my," but "us and ours." All you have and all you are is invested in the marriage union as two become one in every aspect.

You Must Embrace a Mutual Biblical View of Money:

Read the following verses and write down what each of them say about wealth:

1. "Yours, O lord, is the greatness and the power and the glory and the victory and the majesty, indeed everything that is in the heavens and the earth; Yours is the dominion, O lord, and You exalt Yourself as head over all. "Both riches and honor *come* from You, and You rule over all, and in Your hand is power and might; and it lies in Your hand

to make great and to strengthen everyone."[3] _____

_____

_____

2. "The earth is the lord's, and all it contains, The world, and those who dwell in it."[4] _____

_____

_____

3. "'The silver is Mine and the gold is Mine,' declares the lord of hosts."[5]

_____

_____

4. "But you shall remember the lord your God, for it is He who is giving you power to make wealth, that He may confirm His covenant which He swore to your fathers, as *it is* this day."[6] _____

_____

_____

5. "He who loves money will not be satisfied with money, nor he who loves abundance *with its* income. This too is vanity."[7] _____

_____

_____

6. "For we have brought nothing into the world, so we cannot take anything out of it either."[8] _____

_____

_____

7. "Neither their silver nor their gold will be able to deliver them On the day of the lord's wrath; And all the earth will be devoured In the fire of His jealousy, For He will make a complete end, Indeed a terrifying one, Of all the inhabitants of the earth."[9] _____

_____

_____

3. 1 Chronicles 29:11–12 (NASB)
4. Psalms 24:1 (NASB)
5. Haggai 2:8 (NASB)
6. Deuteronomy 8:18 (NASB)
7. Ecclesiastes 5:10 (NASB)
8. 1 Timothy 6:7 (NASB)
9. Zephaniah 1:18 (NASB)

8. "Thus I hated all the fruit of my labor for which I had labored under the sun, for I must leave it to the man who will come after me. And who knows whether he will be a wise man or a fool? Yet he will have control over all the fruit of my labor for which I have labored by acting wisely under the sun. This too is vanity."[10] _____

_____

_____

Biblical Truths Concerning Wealth:

- God owns everything.
- It is God who enables you to work and acquire wealth.
- The person who loves money will never be satisfied.
- Money cannot save your life.
- You cannot take your wealth with you when you die.
- All of the fruit of your labor will be left for someone else's enjoyment—he may be wise or a fool who may spend it all.

You Must Recognize and Avoid Financial Pitfalls:

A prudent man sees danger and takes refuge, but the simple keep going and suffer for it.[11]

1. What does it mean to be prudent? _____

_____

_____

2. The text says a prudent man does two things as he journeys through life; he sees danger and takes refuge. What does the writer mean when he says that "a prudent man sees danger?" _____

_____

_____

10. Ecclesiastes 2:18–19 (NASB)
11. Proverbs 22:3 (NIV)

3. What are some of the possible dangers as it relates to finances, money, and wealth? _____

_____

_____

4. What does a prudent man do when he sees danger? He takes refuge. What does it mean to "take refuge?" _____

_____

_____

5. What is the anticipated outcome of a person who takes cover when he is facing danger? _____

_____

_____

6. On the other hand, Proverbs 22:3 says that the simple man does just the opposite of the prudent man. How would you define a simple person? _____

_____

_____

7. A simple person sees the same danger as the prudent but keeps on going. What does it to mean to "keep on going" when you see a stop sign in plain view of a police officer? _____

_____

_____

8. How does the phrase "keep on going" relate to how the simple may respond to financial dangers? _____

_____

_____

9. What is the fate of a simple person who sees dangers, yet keeps on going? _____

_____

_____

Here are Some Possible Dangers that you Should be on the Lookout for and Take Refuge from:

- Co-signing on debts.[12]

- Covetousness.[13]

- Credit cards: the high-interest rate in small print.[14]

- Discontentment.[15]

- Envy.[16]

- Gambling or lottery tickets.[17]

- Get rich quick schemes, including "Pyramid schemes."[18]

- Greed.[19]

- Laziness.[20]

- Materialism.[21]

- Overspending.[22]

- Payday loans.[23]

- Poor stewardship.[24]

- Repossessions and foreclosures.[25]

You can avoid falling into financial pitfalls by being a prudent person who is circumspect (who looks around with caution) and sees financial dangers,

12. Proverbs 17:18 (NASB)

13. Exodus 20:17; Acts 20:33 (NASB)

14. Proverbs 22:7 (NASB)

15. Ecclesiastes 5:10–11; Philippians 4:11–13 (NASB)

16. Psalms 73 (NASB)

17. Luke 16:13–14 (NASB)

18. Proverbs 13:11, 28:20 (NASB)

19. Ecclesiastes 6:7; Luke 12:15 (NASB)

20. Proverbs 6:6–11 (NASB)

21. Ecclesiastes 2:1–11 (NASB)

22. Luke 12:15, 15:11–32 (NASB)

23. Proverbs 22:7 (NASB)

24. Luke 16:10 (NASB)

25. Proverbs 22:26–27 (NASB)

considers all the options, and takes refuge. Do not be simple and keep going in the face of danger. If you do, you and your family will suffer!

If you are guilty of falling into avoidable financial pitfalls, you must confess, repent, and seek God's forgiveness. Start fresh by seeking refuge and developing a recovery plan.

You Must Work Together in Developing a Plan of Refuge for Managing Finances:

A prudent man sees danger and takes refuge, but the simple keep going and suffer for it.[26]

I moved into my first apartment when I was a nineteen-year-old young man. For me, leaving home to live independent of my mother was an exciting experience. However, I learned early-on that I was terrible at managing my money. I lived paycheck to paycheck. My roommate Rex and I were co-workers at the Hyatt Hotel. Rex was a few years older than I was and more mature. We did not have checking accounts. ATMs and debit cards were not used at that time. Neither of us owned a car, so public transportation was our primary means of getting to and from work. Sometimes I borrowed money from my roommate, who always seemed to have an abundance. On a few occasions, Rex advised me to keep saving, but his advice was ignored.

Eight months after Rex and I became roommates, the hotel began to cut hours and lay off employees due to a drop in revenue. I struggled during this time because I did not see it coming, so I was unprepared. Our hours at work were cut to three days a week. I was able to pay my share of the rent, but food was scarce. I had to walk to wherever I wanted to go because I did not have bus fare. But for Rex, he lived life as usual, enjoying his favorite food and beverages, going wherever he wanted, and enjoying life. Finally, I reached my breaking point, and I asked Rex what is his secret to managing money. He gave me several points that blessed my life. Here is his advice:

- Always have a savings of some sort so you will have access to cash when you need it.

26. Proverbs 22:3 (NIV)

- Purchase a twenty to fifty-dollar money order every time you receive a paycheck; write your name as the payee, put them away in a safe place, and cash them only when necessary.

- Purchase a monthly Metro bus pass in advance. If you do, you will always have transportation to and from work, even when your funds are low.

- Always keep a supply of non-perishable foods just in case.

- Control your spending habits. Do not spend money, you intend to pay bills with, on pleasure.

- Plan: Set goals for purchasing big-ticket items. Set a little funds aside until you have saved enough to buy what you want so that it does not cause financial stress.

It has been over four decades since Rex and I were roommates. Although it has been years since he gave me wise counsel on managing money, his words of wisdom still resonate with me today. Proverbs gives wise advice: "Without consultation, plans are frustrated, But with many counselors, they succeed."[27]

Early on in my life, I tried managing my finances alone and refused to listen to the wise consultation of my roommate. So when I experienced un-expected financial hardships, many of my plans were shattered. The word "frustrated" in Proverbs 15:22 means annulled, broken, ineffective, nulli-fied, or thwarted. My plans were inadequate, broken, and canceled because of poor financial management and my refusal to accept counsel. However, by adhering to the consultation and advice of my roommate, I learned how to develop a plan of refuge that helped me do a much better job managing my finances.

How can you and your spouse develop a plan of refuge for managing fi-nances? _____

_____

_____

Read the following verses and write what each says about managing finances, including budgeting, savings, contentment, investment, seeking counsel, spending, paying for repairs, planning, debt, paying taxes, covet-ing, loans, credit cards, and co-signing:

27. Proverbs 15:22 (NASB)

1. "The graven images of their gods you are to burn with fire; you shall not covet the silver or the gold that is on them, nor take it for yourselves, or you will be snared by it, for it is an abomination to the lord your God."[28] _____

   _____

   _____

2. "Do not withhold good from those to whom it is due, When it is in your power to do *it*. Do not say to your neighbor, 'Go, and come back, And tomorrow I will give *it*,' When you have it with you."[29] _____

   _____

   _____

3. "Where there is no guidance the people fall, But in abundance of counselors there is victory."[30] _____

   _____

   _____

4. "He who is guarantor for a stranger will surely suffer for it, But he who hates being a guarantor is secure."[31] _____

   _____

   _____

5. "The rich rules over the poor, And the borrower *becomes* the lender's slave."[32] _____

   _____

   _____

6. "By wisdom a house is built, And by understanding it is established; And by knowledge the rooms are filled With all precious and pleasant riches."[33] _____

   _____

   _____

28. Deuteronomy 7:25 (NASB)
29. Proverbs 3:27–28 (NASB)
30. Proverbs 11:14 (NASB)
31. Proverbs 11:15 (NASB)
32. Proverbs 22:7 (NASB)
33. Proverbs 24:3–4 (NASB)

7. "For *it is* just like a man *about* to go on a journey, who called his own slaves and entrusted his possessions to them. To one he gave five talents, to another, two, and to another, one, each according to his own ability; and he went on his journey. Immediately the one who had received the five talents went and traded with them and gained five more talents. In the same manner the one who *had received* the two *talents* gained two more. But he who received the one *talent* went away and dug *a hole* in the ground and hid his master's money."[34] _____

_____

_____

8. "For which one of you, when he wants to build a tower, does not first sit down and calculate the cost to see if he has enough to complete it? Otherwise, when he has laid a foundation and is not able to finish, all who observe it begin to ridicule him"[35] _____

_____

_____

9. "Therefore, it is necessary to be in subjection, not only because of wrath, but also for conscience' sake. For because of this you also pay taxes, for *rulers* are servants of God, devoting themselves to this very thing. Render to all what is due them: tax to whom tax *is due;* custom to whom custom; fear to whom fear; honor to whom honor."[36] _____

_____

_____

10. "But if anyone does not provide for his own, and especially for those of his household, he has denied the faith and is worse than an unbeliever."[37] _____

_____

_____

11. "But godliness *is* a means of great gain when accompanied by contentment."[38] _____

_____

_____

34. Matthew 25:14–28 (NASB)
35. Luke 14:28–29 (NASB)
36. Romans 13:5–7 (NASB)
37. 1 Timothy 5:8 (NASB)
38. 1 Timothy 6:6 (NASB)

You Must Honor God with Your Wealth:

> Honor the lord with your wealth and with the best part of every-
> thing you produce. Then he will fill your barns with grain, and
> your vats will overflow with good wine.[39]

Honor means to glorify, to be pleasing to. Honor the lord—Yahweh—He is
"The I am, that I am." The self-existing one, supreme authority, and ruler.
He is the one who was, who is, and who always will be. The one who owns
everything. The master and lord.

Honor God With What?

- With Your Wealth: Substance, riches, and possession.
- With the best part of everything that you produce—gains, revenue,
  earnings, and profits—the best of what you receive now and obtain in
  the future.

How can You Honor God with Your Wealth?

- Put God first: Make the things of God your priority. Trust God, sub-
  mit to Jesus as Lord, and live a life pleasing to God by practicing righ-
  teousness and conforming to the likeness of Christ.[40]
- Practice good stewardship.[41]
- Giving to the poor.[42]
- Tithing and giving.[43]
- Using your possessions to bless others.[44]

39. Proverbs 3:9–10 (NLT2)
40. Matthew 6:33 (NASB)
41. Matthew 25:21 (NASB)
42. Deuteronomy 15:11; Proverbs 14:31, 19:17; Matthew 25:31–45 (NASB)
43. 2 Corinthians 9:6–9 (NASB)
44. Luke 3:11; James 2:14–17 (NASB)

How can you use what you own to be a blessing to others?

- Supporting the kingdom: mission work.[45]

- Giving to homeless shelters.

- Giving to church building funds.

- Community services: nursing homes, schools, mentoring programs, etc.

> Then he will fill your barns with grain, and your vats will overflow with good wine.[46]

You do not have barns or wine vats, but what does Proverbs 3:10 say happens when you honor God with your wealth? _____

_____

_____

God's blessings of having abundance should never be your motive for honoring God with your wealth. God's blessings are the by-product of honoring God with your wealth, not the motivation. If God does not bless you with anything else, he has already blessed you enough.

> But godliness *is* a means of great gain when accompanied by contentment.[47]

A Dollar Speaks:

Money talks, we have been told since childhood. Listen to this dollar speak: "You hold me in your hand and call me yours. Yet may I not as well call you mine. See how easily I rule you? To gain me, you would all but die. I am invaluable as rain, essential as water. Without me, men and institutions would die. Yet I do not hold the power of life for them; I am futile without the stamp of your desire. I go nowhere unless you send me. I keep strange company. For me, men mock, love, and scorn character. Yet, I am appointed to the service of saints, to give education to the growing mind and food to

45. 2 Corinthians 9:10–15 (NASB)
46. Proverbs 3:10 (NLT2)
47. 1 Timothy 6:6 (NASB)

the starving bodies of the poor. My power is terrific. Handle me carefully and wisely, lest you become my servant, rather than I yours."[48]

Conclusion:

The purpose of this chapter is to provide you and your fiancée or spouse with a biblical view of money and wealth. These principles are essential for helping you and your spouse establish and maintain oneness amid differing views of finances so that you can avoid the unnecessary misery and difficulties that often occur as a result of the unbiblical view and mismanagement of money. We challenge you to employ these biblical truths in your life and your marriage. In doing so, you will establish oneness as it relates to finances. More importantly, as you commit to being good stewards of God's provisions by honoring the Lord with your money, your marriage will be overflowing with an abundance of God's blessings. Remember, money and wealth—in and of itself—is not evil. It is the love of money and wealth that is a sin. The love of wealth facilitates evil and is displeasing to God.

Application Discussion Questions:

1. What is your annual gross income? _____
   _____
   _____

2. What is your fiancée or spouse's gross monthly income? _____
   _____
   _____

3. How much debt do you currently have?

Credit cards:	
Student loans:	

---

48. Tan, Paul Lee. *Encyclopedia of 7700 Illustrations: A Treasury of Illustrations, Anecdotes, Facts, and Quotations for Pastors, Teachers, and Christian Workers*. Garland: Bible Communications, 1996. (page 823)

Mortgage:	
Auto:	
Other:	

4. How much debt does your fiancée or spouse currently have?

Credit cards:	
Student loans:	
Mortgage:	
Auto:	
Other:	

5. Do you and your fiancée or spouse have any of the following insurance policies, and if so, what is the amount of coverage and the amount of the monthly premiums?

Insurance type:	Him:	Her:
Auto:		
Life:		
Medical:		
Dental:		
Long-term care:		

6. Who and how will you manage the finances once you get married? __
   _____
   _____

7. How much of your earnings or wealth are you willing to entrust in your marriage union? _____
   _____
   _____

8. Should you and your spouse have joint bank accounts; why or why not? _____
   _____
   _____

9. How will decisions be made when it comes to making large purchases?
   _____
   _____

10. How will you handle family members who ask for financial assistance?
    _____
    _____

11. Are you planning to continue your education sometime in the future?
    _____
    _____

    If so, how will that be financed? _____
    _____
    _____

    Will your spouse be able to support the household on one income? __
    _____
    _____

    Do you plan to continue to working and attend school part-time? ___
    _____
    _____
    _____

12. Is your spouse or fiancee aware of any of your investments such as 401k, stocks, savings accounts, bonds, mutual funds, SEPs, or personal property that you own? _____

_____

_____

13. How will the finances be managed if the wife becomes pregnant and unable to work for several months? _____

_____

_____

Sample Monthly Budget:

Add your monthly income:

Your income _____

Your spouse's income _____

Other income _____

Total _____

Plan your expenses:

Rent or mortgage _____

Utilities _____

Food _____

Auto _____

Insurance _____

Giving or tithes _____

Savings _____

Memberships _____

Entertainment _____

Other _____

Total _____

Adjust your expenses wherever possible so that they do not exceed your monthly income. Use credit cards only for emergency purchases, and if possible, pay your full credit card balance within 30 days to avoid interest.

13

Raising Children

Reaching the Heart of Your Children

Counseling Issue:

LARRY AND JULIE ARE a blended family and have been married for four years. They have a three-year-old son together, and Julie has a ten-year-old daughter, Susan, from a previous marriage. Larry told Susan on several occasions to complete her homework when she gets home from school, clean her room, and then she can watch television or play video games. He arrived home one evening and found Susan playing video games. Her room was dirty, and she did not complete her homework. As he began to admonish her, she yelled at him, saying, "you are not my father!" Larry gave her a mild spanking and sent her to her room.

When Julie arrived home that evening, she was met at the door by Susan pleading her case and describing, in an exaggerated fashion, how Larry spanked her. Larry attempted to explain the situation, but before he could finish his sentence, Julie screamed at him, saying, "Keep your hands off of my child!" From that time on, Larry refused to discipline Susan. By the time Susan reached seventeen years old, she was rebellious and out of control. When they discovered that Susan was pregnant, Julie and Susan got into a heated argument as Larry stood and watched. During this exchange, Julie then turned to Larry and shouted, "are you just going to stand there and say nothing?" Larry replied, "That is between the two of you. I removed my hands years ago."

Counseling Issue:

Brenda is a single mother who is having trouble with her oldest teenage son. Whenever she attempts to discipline him for malicious behavior, she always experiences some form of resistance. Her son is combative and argumentative. He talks back and shows no respect for her. Often, when she asks him to clean his room, or wash the dishes, he either smirks or moves like a turtle. When she says something that he does not like, he walks away as she is talking. She tries to guide him and teach him lessons about life, but he claims to know it all. When she tries to discipline him, he accuses her of loving his younger brother more than him. Finally, Brenda reaches her wits end and decides to give up trying. Whenever she attempts to correct him, and he opposes her, she stops talking to him, sometimes for several days. She is now emotionally and mentally exhausted.

Counseling Issue:

Pastor Scott and his wife, Sandra, have three sons. They have always taught their children Christian values. Paul works to fulfill his pastoral duties and is also a devoted father who loves his sons. The boys are smart and highly involved in youth church activities. Timothy, the oldest, graduated high school and went off to college. During his third year, Paul received a phone call from Timothy. Paul was glad to hear his son's voice, however, as Timothy spoke, it was easy to tell that something was wrong. So Paul asked, "Son, are you okay?" Then Timothy said something that shocked Paul and cut to the core of his heart. Timothy said, "I am an atheist, Dad!" Paul shared the conversation with his wife and they cried together in disbelief. They could not understand how, after years of dedicating their life to raising their son in a Christian home, their son could suddenly deny God's existence.

The Problem:

Larry and Julie: A parent's or stepparent's failure to exercise God-ordained authority over their children will result in rebellion.

Brenda: A parent who allows herself to be manipulated, disrespected, and controlled by her son is one who suffers the consequences of sparing the rod and the lack of administering age-appropriate discipline.

Paul and Sandra: Parents wrongly believe that children raised in a Christian home will never go astray. Teaching Christian values in the home do not guarantee righteous children.

Objective:

The purpose of this chapter is to help couples understand and fulfill their biblical roles as parents. They will learn principles of parenting children, raising them in the fear and admonition of the Lord. The primary focus of parents, from a biblical perspective, is exposing and transforming the hearts of their children through the gospel of Christ. Couples will learn how to address the sinful nature of their children by addressing the sinful inclinations of their hearts and help them know God's grace and the salvation of Jesus Christ through the gospel.

Parents are called to exercise God-ordained authority by shepherding their children, training them in righteousness, instructing about life and living. This includes disciplining, counseling, and encouraging their children on how to glorify and love God and others.

Teenagers: From Tranquility to Turmoil:

During the eighteenth and nineteenth centuries, corporal punishment, including spanking, was allowed in public schools across America. In fact, during the 1950s, corporal punishment was not only permissible to teachers but neighbors as well. Your teacher could spank you for misbehavior. The neighbor could paddle you if they saw you doing something wrong. And when your parents found out what you did, you would receive another spanking when they got home. Children addressed every adult person that they met as "sir" or "ma'am." Anything less was disrespectful. Most kids viewed all adults as authorities. Those who happened to walk by a church temporarily corrected their bad behavior as an expression of respect to God and the church, even if they were unbelievers. Respecting one's superiors was a significant part of our culture.

In today's culture, some say teenagers are out of control. Many teens lack respect for authority. A child who can give full reign to the sinful and wicked desires of his heart will spiral downward in self-destruction. He will also become a burden to others because he is hard to deal with. A child who is disrespectful to his parents will also be disrespectful to his teachers. He will more than likely be combative with a police officer. As an adult, if left unrepentant, he or she will exhibit the same malicious behavior with bosses, other authorities, in college, and in marriage. A child who is out of control will grow up to be an unrestrained out-of-control adult.

Road rage, violent crime, school shootings, and domestic violence are the results of someone who is out of control. Undisciplined children usually grow up having no respect for authority. More importantly, if they have no respect for God-ordained authority, then they will have no respect for God and his word. The fate of an undisciplined child is misery, incarceration, or a life that is cut short.

So, what is your role as a parent? How can you help your children live a prosperous and successful life? You can do so by raising your children in the fear and admonition of the Lord. Your children must be taught to respect God-ordained authority. You must view your children as sinners just like you are. The target is not merely addressing your children's behavior—you must address the heart issues at the root of your children's behavior. What anger, fear, desire, shame, guilt, envy, coveting, or withholding forgiveness is at the root if the sinful behavior? You and your spouse or a counselor can discover what issues need to be addressed.

Parents are a God-ordained Authority:

Since marriage was created to reflect the image of God, in terms of oneness, love, grace, goodness, and mercy, marriage is also created to reflect God's dominion and authority. God-ordained authorities are those individuals that God placed in a position of authority. All Christians are called to submit to superiors. A child's first encounter with God's authority is through his parents. The only exception to submitting to God-ordained authority is if a superior requires you to violate God's word.

The Bible identifies five positions of God-ordained authority. Read the following scripture, identify, and write down who is the God-ordained authority is each passage:

1. "Every person is to be in subjection to the governing authorities. For there is no authority except from God, and those which exist are established by God. Therefore, whoever resists authority has opposed the ordinance of God; and they who have opposed will receive condemnation upon themselves."[1] _____

   _____

2. "Servants [workers] be submissive to your masters [overseers] with all respect, not only to those who are good and gentle, but also to those who are unreasonable. For this *finds* favor, if for the sake of conscience toward God a person bears up under sorrows when suffering unjustly."[2] _____

   _____

3. "Wives, *be subject* to your own husbands, as to the Lord. For the husband is the head of the wife, as Christ also is the head of the church, He Himself *being* the Savior of the body. But as the church is subject to Christ, so also the wives *ought to be* to their husbands in everything."[3]

   _____

4. "Obey your leaders and submit *to them,* for they keep watch over your souls as those who will give an account. Let them do this with joy and not with grief, for this would be unprofitable for you."[4] _____

   _____

5. "But we request of you, brethren, that you appreciate those who diligently labor among you, and have charge over you in the Lord and give you instruction"[5] _____

   _____

1. Romans 13:1–2 (NASB)
2. 1 Peter 2:18–19 (NASB)
3. Ephesians 5:22–24 (NASB)
4. Hebrews 13:17 (NASB)
5. 1 Thessalonians 5:12 (NASB)

6. "Children be obedient to your parents in all things, for this is well-pleasing to the Lord."[6] _____

_____

_____

Governmental officials (including police officers), employers, husbands, church leaders, and parents are all God-ordained authorities. You must establish and exercise your authority over your children. Here is a warning! You will have difficulty exercising authority if your child views you and relates to you as one of their peers. Sure, it is essential to relate, listen to, and connect with your children to some degree on their level. However, you cannot view yourself as a friend of your children. You must not give them complete freedom to do or say whatever they want so you can remain friendly with them or so they will like you. Also, you can not relate to your young children as equals, treat them as adults, or expect that they will think, respond, and behave as an adult would. Instead, you must enforce your parental authority out of love for them and in obedience to what God has called you to do as a parent. As you exercise your authority, continually remind your children of their position and your expectation of respectful obedience to your authority.

Parents are the Trainers of the Children:

Every professional sports team has a coach and possibly an assistant coach. The coach's responsibility is to lead the team to victory through intensive training. Most training involves instruction, conditioning, preparation, and discipline. Training can be divided into two elements: teaching and discipline. The common problem in coaching is that every player is different. Each player has his own set of strengths and weaknesses. Therefore, a good coach, with assistance, must structure and modify his training so that it fits the needs of each player. As each player's abilities are developed, the team improves as a whole. As the team engages each opponent, the coach cheers them on. He is the encourager. If the team loses, he encourages them to do better the next time. One of my coach's words of encouragement at every practice was, "I am not expecting you to be great. I want you to do better today than you did yesterday."

6. Colossians 3:20 (NASB)

Being a parent is being a coach. Your goal is to help your children become the best that they can be. To accomplish this task, you must teach and discipline your children. The challenge is that all children have their own set of strengths and weaknesses. Therefore, you may have to modify your training and instruction to fit the strengths and weaknesses of each child. Some parents make the mistake of attempting to train each child the same way.

Read the following scriptures and answer the corresponding questions for each passage.

> Train up a child in the way he should go, Even when he is old he will not depart from it.[7]

1. What do you think the phrase, "Train up a child," means? _____
   _____
   _____

2. According to Proverbs 22:6, each child needs training on "the way he should go." What do you think this means, and is it the same for each child; why or why not? Which ways should be the same; which ones may be different? _____
   _____
   _____

3. The verse says, "even when he is old, he will not depart from it." Is the word "old" referring to age or maturity? What does it mean to depart from something? _____
   _____
   _____

> My son, do not reject the discipline of the lord or loathe His reproof, For whom the lord loves He reproves, Even as a father *corrects* the son in whom he delights.[8]

4. According to Proverbs 3:11–12, whom does the Lord discipline? ____
   _____
   _____

7. Proverbs 22:6 (NASB)
8. Proverbs 3:11–12 (NASB)

5. What reason must be kept in view when we discipline? _____

_____

_____

> Fathers, do not provoke your children to anger, but bring them up in the discipline and instruction of the Lord.[9]

6. As you consider Proverbs 3:11–12 and Ephesians 6:4, why must discipline and instruction of the Lord go hand in hand? _____

_____

_____

> Then David said to his son Solomon, "Be strong and courageous, and act; do not fear nor be dismayed, for the lord God, my God, is with you. He will not fail you nor forsake you until all the work for the service of the house of the lord is finished."[10]

7. Children need encouragement. In 1 Chronicles 28:20, how does King David encourage his son Solomon? _____

_____

_____

8. What does he tell Solomon to do? _____

_____

_____

9. What does he tell Solomon not to do? _____

_____

_____

10. What motivation did David give Solomon for following his instructions and how was it encouraging for Solomon to know? _____

_____

_____

Parents are their children's trainers. It involves encouragement and motivation. You are your child's Coach and coaching also requires teaching and discipline. The Bible is replete with instructions about discipline. Those

9. Ephesians 6:4 (NASB)
10. 1 Chronicles 28:20 (NASB)

who spare the rod of discipline hate their children. Those who love their children care enough to discipline them.[11]

> Foolishness is bound up in the heart of a child; The rod of discipline will remove it far from him.[12]

> Do not withhold discipline from a child; if you punish him with the rod, he will not die.[13]

Proverbs 22:6 says, "Train up a child in the way he should go, even when he is old, he will not depart from it." A proverb, or maxim is a short, pithy, and wise saying and a general truth or code of conduct, intentionally written in a way to make it memorable. The Proverbs are general truths that hold true in most cases, but not all.

This proverb is one of the most misused and misunderstood passages often quoted by the church. Most people use this verse to validate the assumption that children who grow up to become wayward as young adults are the direct result of a parent's lack of discipline and training. They blame disobedience and defiance on the parent. In many cases, this statement is true. However, Proverbs 22:6 is not merely speaking of teaching children godly principles. Training your children in the way they should go, in this Scripture, is referring to training them according to their natural bent. Each child's natural inclination is toward sin, so the way that they would go, without training, would lean toward sin and waywardness. Since each child's weaknesses and heart sensitivities may be different, your training should be what each child is capable of and will not necessarily be the same for each child.

Consider the story of the pastor in the introduction of this chapter. Training up a child "in the way that he should go, and he will not depart from it" is right in a general sense but does not always hold true in every instance. A child can be raised by godly parents who give instruction and discipline of the Lord, and yet as a young adult, that child can still go wayward. Proper godly training of your children can facilitate obedience, and produce well-behaved, and responsible adults. It can be hoped that they will not depart from righteous teaching, but it does always preclude waywardness. Many young adults have strayed from the godly training they received as a child. Yet early training and instruction in the ways of the

11. Proverbs 13:24 (NLT2)
12. Proverbs 22:15 (NASB)
13. Proverbs 23:13 (NIV)

Lord will be of great gain in their repentance and getting on back the right path. Parents can be comforted by the fact that they have done what they are commanded to do according to God's word.

Parents are the Counselors of their Children:

What is a biblical counselor? A biblical counselor gives hope, compassionately identifies heart issues in their counselee then helps them to recognize and confess sin, seek God's forgiveness, and practice repentance. The counselor then offers practical theology. Practical theology involves instruction and application of God's word to everyday life and living. A biblical counselor helps others to grow in their understanding of God, oneself, relationships, and how to respond to unfavorable situations, circumstances, and events.

Too many parents make the mistake of focusing on their child's behavior without addressing their heart issues. The heart is what drives thoughts and behavior. As a parent, you must be aware of the condition of your children's hearts. What are their struggles? What are their fears? What are their idols? How are they handling peer pressure? How do they relate to others? What challenges are they facing? Who are their friends? Once you identify these issues can you relate to what they are experiencing. Have you ever struggled with the same problems?

Read the following scriptures and answer the corresponding questions at it relates to counseling others:

> A plan in the heart of a man is *like* deep water, But a man of understanding draws it out.[14]

1. A plan in the heart of man consist of his thoughts, will, intentions, and motives. But a man of discernment draws it out. What are some ways you can draw out the thoughts, intentions, and motives of a child? ___

   _____

   _____

> Spouting off before listening to the facts is both shameful and foolish.[15]

14. Proverbs 20:5 (NASB)
15. Proverbs 18:13 (NLT2)

2. According to Proverbs 18:13, what is the result of giving an answer before hearing all the facts; what can you do to avoid it? _____

_____

_____

3. What is it that keeps parents from listening to their children? _____

_____

_____

> Brethren, even if anyone is caught in any trespass, you who are spiritual, restore such a one in a spirit of gentleness; *each one* looking to yourself, so that you too will not be tempted.[16]

4. When your child commits a sin or does something wrong, how should you respond according to Galatians 6:1? Why must you also examine your own propensity to error, and how you would want to be corrected? _____

_____

_____

> We urge you, brethren, admonish the unruly, encourage the fainthearted, help the weak, be patient with everyone.[17]

5. In Thessalonians 5:14, the writer gives us three sets of counseling instructions for addressing three kinds of people. The unruly: the disorderly, disobedient, and undisciplined; those who are out of line. The fainthearted: those who are worried, distressed, discouraged, disappointed, or losing heart. The weak: without strength, powerless, doubting, or weak in faith (the simple, naive, and inexperienced child can be considered vulnerable and easily influenced by the world). Paul says the unruly needs to be admonished. What does admonish mean?

_____

_____

6. Paul says the fainthearted needs to be encouraged. What does the word "encourage" mean? _____

_____

_____

---

16. Galatians 6:1 (NASB)
17. 1 Thessalonians 5:14 (NASB)

7. Paul says the weak needs to be helped. What does it mean to help the weak? _____

_____

_____

8. Paul says no matter what the condition of man is, be patient with all. Be patient with the unruly, the fainthearted, and the weak. What harm do you think it will bring to your child if you admonish them for their weakness or discourage them when they are disappointed? _____

_____

_____

Words of Encouragement and Caution as You Seek to Counsel Your Children:

Your counsel will be ineffective if your children refuse to talk to you. Most parents want their children to talk, to be open, and share their struggles. Parents never want to see their children suffer, but too many parents are impatient with their teenagers. We cut-off our children while they are talking because the child's views and responses sound like foolishness. We will shut down our children because what the child is saying does not align with logical thinking. We fail to realize that children speak and share information based upon their own worldview. It is unrealistic to expect a child's thinking and conception of the world to align with yours as someone over twice their age. It is certainly irrational for parents to become agitated and angry because their children cannot comprehend their wise counsel.

As you seek to counsel your children, you must be mindful that children think and speak as children. Scripture says, "When I was a child, I used to speak like a child, think like a child, reason like a child; when I became a man, I did away with childish things."[18] Recognize that your children are sinners in need of forgiveness and the salvation of our Lord, Jesus Christ. The same grace that covers you is the same grace that covers them upon the confession of their faith in Christ. Except for presenting the Gospel and the saving grace of Christ, counseling a child who is not redeemed will not differ from counseling a child who is redeemed. Those who are saved from God's wrath are still capable of sin.

18. 1 Corinthians 13:11 (NASB)

Be mindful that sinners tend to manipulate others for selfish reasons. Selfishness is an issue of the heart that must be exposed. Here are a few common examples of how children attempt to manipulate their parents:

- You are forced to repeat yourself before your child follows your instructions.
- Your child often asks "why" when he is told to do something.
- You withhold discipline because your child talks you out of it.
- You find yourself always having to defend your position or decisions.
- Your child continues to beg and plead for something that she wants even after you have said no.
- Your child repeatedly has an excuse for failing to meet your expectations.
- When you attempt to discipline your child, he plays on your emotions by accusing you of loving other siblings more than him.
- Your child apologizes for wrongdoing, then in the next breath, asks for something he wants.[19]

Establish a code of conduct for such manipulation. Bring to the child's awareness your discernment of what they are attempting to do. Communicate your expectations, enforce the rules, and the consequences of breaking the rules—and stick to it! Do not vacillate. Be consistent. If you are inconstant, your child will continue to be manipulative because they will not take you seriously.

Parents are not to Provoke their Children to Wrath:

Have you ever been provoked to anger? A boss can incite you to anger by overlooking you for a job promotion when he gives it to someone less-experienced. A spouse can provoke you to anger by the offensive things they say to you. Neighbors can trigger rage in you when they allow their dogs to bark all night. Drivers can provoke you to anger when they cut you off on the road. Children can provoke you to irritation when you find out they are dishonest. Friends can provoke you to anger when they share information about you (that you deemed confidential) with others.

---

19. Priolo, *The Heart of Anger*, 122.

When people provoke you to anger, it does not justify your anger or make it permissible. People can let you down and offend you. You learn to forgive and chose not to remember it. Then you move on with life. However, nothing can be more tragic and more devastating than when parents provoke their children to anger. Provoking a young child to anger is usually not something they get over as an adult. It can have lasting effects. Adult children may choose to retaliate as parents get older. They may decide to retaliate by preventing parents from seeing grandchildren. Visits with parents can become less and less frequent. Some adult children who are provoked to anger may become physical or verbally abusive to their aging, sick parents. They may even refuse to care for them and relinquish their responsibility to someone else. Provocation never makes this type of behavior right. A parent's confession, repentance, and forgiveness from the child can repair the child's wounded heart and reconcile the relationship.

Read the following text and answer the corresponding questions:

> Fathers, do not provoke your children to anger, but bring them up in the discipline and instruction of the Lord.[20]

1. The principles in Ephesians 6:4 also apply to a mother. But why do you believe Paul mentions fathers only and not the mother? _____
   _____
   _____

2. What are some ways a parent can provoke their children to anger? ____
   _____
   _____

3. The phrase, "bring them up," means to nurture. According to Ephesians 6:4, what is the opposite of provoking your children to anger? __
   _____
   _____

4. What is the discipline of the Lord? What are the consequences of unacceptable behavior? _____
   _____
   _____

20. Ephesians 6:4 (NASB)

5. What is the instruction of the Lord? In other words, what do they need to know about what God requires and about Jesus Christ? _____

_____

_____

Fathers do not exasperate your children so that they will not lose heart.[21]

6. In Colossians 3:21, the word "exasperate" means to stir up to anger, to make resentful, or to make bitter. What are some of the ways a parent can exasperate a child? _____

_____

_____

7. When parents exasperate their children, it causes children to lose heart. What does it mean "to lose heart?" _____

_____

_____

What is it like to give your best to please your parents, but your best is never good enough? Here are some other ways parents provoke or exasperate their children to anger, resentment, and bitterness which causes them to lose heart.

Ways Children Can Be Provoked to Anger or Exasperated:

Comparing your child to others.	Falsely accusing them of lying without reason.
Letting them have their way.	Refusing to praise or encourage.
Lack of discipline.	Name-calling.
Not allowing them to express themselves.	Always pointing-out their faults.
Being insensitive to their feelings.	Admonishing them in public.
Showing favoritism.	Mocking of their inadequacies.

21. Colossians 3:21 (NASB)

If you have failed as a parent, there is always hope. But you must be willing to confess your failures to God first then to your children. It is never too late to do this. Affirm your love to your children. Tell your children precisely how you have failed as a parent. Put the blame squarely on yourself, not on their behavior. Ask your children for their forgiveness. Then, seek to be best father or mother that you can to the glory of God.

Conclusion:

The purpose of this chapter is to help couples understand and fulfill their roles as parents. You are called to raise your children in the fear and admonition of the Lord. This can be accomplished by exposing and transforming the hearts of your children through the gospel of Christ. Parents must address the sinful nature of their children by addressing their hearts and help them know God and the salvation of Jesus Christ. Parents are called to exercise God-ordained authority by training in righteousness, instructing about life and living, discipline, counseling, and encouraging their children on how to glorify and love God and others.

How can parents fulfill their role? You can do so by remembering that:

- Parents are God-ordained authorities.
- Parents are the trainers of their children.
- Parents are the counselors of their children.
- Parents are not to Provoke their children to wrath.

"No man ever really finds out what he believes in until he begins to instruct his children. The best inheritance a parent can give his children is a few minutes of his time each day."

—ANONYMOUS

14

How to Move from Chaos to Conformity in Christ

Christ and Your Marriage:

I am the vine, you are the branches; he who abides in Me and I in him, he bears much fruit, for apart from Me you can do nothing.[1]

God's Design for a Successful Marriage:

Point 1:

THE PURPOSE OF MARRIAGE is to become one flesh. It is a covenant of companionship:[2]

- Created to reflect the image of God.[3]
- Jesus said I and the father are one.[4]
- God is a trinitarian being.[5]

---

1. John 15:5 (NASB95)
2. Genesis 2:18, 23–24 (NASB)
3. Genesis 1:26–27 (NASB)
4. John 10:30 (NASB)
5. Matthew 28:19; 2 Corinthians 13:14 (NASB)

The Problem:

You cannot become one flesh apart from Christ. The Triune God is the model for our relationships. The natural (unsaved) person is only concerned about himself. He or she has the mindset of the individualist who says, "what's mine is mine, and what's yours is yours."

Point 2:

The husband must love his wife as Christ loved the church, and the wife must submit to and respect her husband![6]

- An unbelieving man cannot love his wife as Christ loved the church.[7]
- An unbelieving woman cannot submit and respect her husband as unto the Lord.[8]
- The natural man cannot please God because he is an enemy of God.[9]

The Problem:

A husband cannot love his wife as Christ loved the church, and a wife cannot submit to and respect her husband apart from Christ. The natural man instinctively wants to rule others. Husbands and wives will instinctively fight for authority over one another.

> Then he said to the woman, "I will sharpen the pain of your pregnancy, and in pain you will give birth. And you will desire to control your husband, but he will rule over you."[10]

Point 3:

Husbands and wives are to maintain unity despite differences, unmet expectations, and personal preferences:

6. Ephesians 5:22–32; 1 Peter 2:16—3:7 (NASB)
7. 1 Corinthians 2:14–15 (NASB)
8. 1 Corinthians 2:14–15; Ephesians 5:22 (NASB)
9. Romans 5:6–11; Ephesians 2:1–10 (NASB)
10. Genesis 3:16 (NLT2)

- Both husbands and wives have value even though they are wired differently.[11]
- Husbands and wives must realize that their spouses will not always meet their expectations.[12]
- Husbands and wives must be willing to accept differences of opinion and personal preferences.[13]
- Husbands and wives must value their spouse as more important than themselves.[14]

The Problem:

A husband and wife cannot accept their differences, unmet expectation, or personal preferences apart from Christ. The natural man is unwilling to accept differences and respond properly to unmet expectations because he is only concerned about himself. He believes his opinion is the only one that matters.

> A loner is out to get what he wants for himself. He opposes all sound reasoning. A fool does not find joy in understanding but only in expressing his own opinion.[15]

Point 4:

Husbands and wives must establish and maintain good communication:[16]

- Believers are commanded to be open and honest and lovingly communicate words that edify the hearer.
- Good communication is not only about sharing your thoughts and concerns, but a sincere attempt to understand the other person.

11. 1 Corinthians 12:12–26 (NASB)
12. Jeremiah 17:5–9; Psalms 13:12 (NASB)
13. Proverbs 18:1–2; 1 Corinthians 12:12–26 (NASB)
14. Philippians 2:3–4 (NASB)
15. Proverbs 18:2 (GW)
16. Ephesians 4:15, 25, 29–32 (NASB)

- The heart of the unbeliever is deceitful and wicked.[17]
- The natural man speaks of that which fills the heart.[18]
- The fool does not delight in understanding but only in giving his own opinion; what he has to say is the only thing that matters.[19]

The Problem:

Husbands and wives cannot exhibit good communication (as God defines good) apart from Christ. [20]They must talk with purpose and listen with understanding. The natural person is only concerned about being understood rather than understanding and speaks that which fills the evilness of his heart.

Point 5:

Husbands and wives must resolve conflict in a godly way to maintain unity:

- Husbands and wives are naturally different in many ways.
- Differences are simply occasions for conflict and are not the source of conflict.
- Conflict occurs when desires become demands. It is an unloving response to not getting what we want or getting what we don't want.[21]
- Conflict can be resolved when you consider your spouse as more important than yourself.[22]
- Conflict can be resolved when you seek to understand your spouse by being a good listener.[23]

17. Jeremiah 17:9 (NASB)
18. Matthew 12:34 (NASB)
19. Proverbs 18:1–2 (NASB)
20. Ephesians 4:29–32 (NASB)
21. James 4:1–3 (NASB)
22. Philippians 2:3–4 (NASB)
23. James 1:19 (NASB)

- Conflict can be resolved when you and spouse confess your sins to one another, seeking, and granting forgiveness.[24]

The Problem:

Husbands and wives cannot biblically resolve conflict apart from Christ. The natural person pursues pleasure and will argue and fight for the fulfillment of selfish desires. His or her desires are for their own benefit, not the benefit of another person.

> What is the source of quarrels and conflicts among you? Is not the source your pleasures that wage war in your members? You lust and do not have; so you commit murder. You are envious and cannot obtain; so you fight and quarrel. You do not have because you do not ask. You ask and do not receive, because you ask with wrong motives, so that you may spend it on your pleasures.[25]

Point 6:

Husbands and wives are to cultivate intimacy:

- Physical intimacy, in general, occurs when a husband and wife are physically connected (it includes touching, kissing, hugging, or holding hands).
- Sexual intimacy is about giving of yourself to your spouse for the enjoyment of your spouse as an open expression of love.[26]
- Emotional intimacy occurs when you and your spouse/fiancé develop a deep affection for one another. You become emotionally connected with your partner when you feel what they feel, hurt when they hurt, and rejoice when they rejoice.[27]

---

24. Matthew 7:1–5; Ephesians 4:22 (NASB)
25. James 4:1–3 (NASB)
26. Hebrews 13:4 (NASB)
27. 1 Peter 3:8 (NASB)

- Mental intimacy happens when you and your spouse become united in heart and mind. It involves the exchange of your thoughts and ideas with respect.[28]

- Spiritual intimacy occurs when a husband and wife are united in Christ and in spirit. They are striving in life together hand in hand, pursuing one purpose, one goal, with one ambition, which is to glorify God.[29]

The Problem:

Marriage is a covenant of companionship, where both the husband and wife are bonded together as one. Husbands and wives must establish and maintain intimacy through the exercising of oneness in every area of their marriage. Husbands and wives cannot experience physical, emotional, mental, and spiritual intimacy apart from Christ.

> The man said, "This is now bone of my bones, And flesh of my flesh; She shall be called Woman, Because she was taken out of Man." For this reason a man shall leave his father and his mother, and be joined to his wife; and they shall become one flesh.[30]

Point 7:

Husbands and wives must establish boundaries with their parents and in-laws and avoid family feuds:

- Husbands and wives must leave their father, mother, and extended family in the following areas: Leave physically: Move out of their parents' home and establish their own dwelling place.[31] Leave financially: Work to earn wages and provide for their household. They must live financially independent of their parents.[32] Leave parental loyalty: Their foremost loyalty is no longer to their parents but to one

28. Philippians 2:1–2 (NASB)
29. 2 Corinthians 5:9 (NASB)
30. Genesis 2:23–24 (NASB)
31. Ephesians 5:31 (NASB)
32. 2 Thessalonians 3:10 (NASB)

another.[33] Leave emotionally: Husbands and wives must learn to work through their relational issues. Parents cannot become an emotional crutch when problems arise. They should not readily share their marital struggles with their parents.[34]

- Husbands and wives must establish boundaries with parents, in-laws, and other relationships outside of the marriage (especially relationships with the opposite sex). Do not allow people to interfere with or cause friction within the marriage.

- Husbands and wives must take time to develop and establish relationships with their new extended family.[35]

- Husbands and wives must resolve personal conflict with in-laws as one adult to another and avoid using the spouse as a go-between. First, seek to resolve the issue one-on-one.[36]

- Husbands and wives must insist that in-laws and extended family members respect their spouse and marriage.

The Problem:

Husbands and wives cannot establish boundaries with parents, in-laws, and people from previous relationships, apart from Christ. The natural man walks in the flesh, willingly engaging in conflict because he is only concerned about himself.

> Now the deeds of the flesh are evident, which are: immorality, impurity, sensuality, idolatry, sorcery, enmities, strife, jealousy, outbursts of anger, disputes, dissensions, factions, envying, drunkenness, carousing, and things like these, of which I forewarn you, just as I have forewarned you, that those who practice such things will not inherit the kingdom of God.[37]

33. Matthew 119:5 (NASB)
34. Matthew 18:15; Galatians 6:1–3 (NASB)
35. Luke 6:31 (NASB)
36. Matthew 18:15; Romans 12:18–21 (NASB)
37. Galatians 5:19–21 (NASB)

Point 8:

Husbands and wives in blended families are to function as a real family:

- The husband and wife's relationship should take precedence over the children.[38]
- A blended family should not be regarded as two separate families co-habitating but as one family.
- Since a husband and father is the God-ordained authority of the home, it is his responsibility to ensure that the children respect and honor him and his wife.[39]
- The new husband and wife must establish a code of conduct for their children and stepchildren.[40]
- Children must honor and respect the stepparent, regardless of their feelings, because it is what God requires of them.[41]

The Problem:

The biggest hurdle that blended families face is trying to establish unity apart from Christ. The natural man's tendency when he or she is in a blended family is to only love those who love them back. They avoid the difficulty of cultivating relationships with resistant children. Parents who put the feelings of their biological children over and above their spouse have violated God's design for marriage and the family.

If a house is divided against itself, that house cannot stand.[42]

Point 9:

Husbands and wives are to be good stewards of their finances:

38. Genesis 2:24 (NASB)
39. Ephesians 6:1–4 (NASB)
40. Colossians 3:18–21 (NASB)
41. Ephesians 6:1–2 (NASB)
42. Mark 3:25 (NIV)

- All the wealth and possessions of the world belong to God.[43]
- God gives us the ability to generate money and wealth.[44]
- You must avoid financial pitfalls.[45]
- You must be a good steward of your finances.[46]
- You must worship God with your wealth.[47]

The Problem:

Husbands and wives must embrace a biblical view of finance and manage their monetary resources in a way that brings honor and glory to God. Husbands and wives cannot maintain unity in the face of abundant wealth or the lack thereof apart from Christ. The natural man is inclined to be a lover of money.

> No one can serve two masters; for either he will hate the one and love the other, or he will be devoted to one and despise the other. You cannot serve God and wealth.[48]

Point 10:

Husbands and wives must practice good parenting skills in raising their children:

- As parents, husbands and wives must exercise their God-ordained authority.[49]
- As parents, husbands and wives must be the biblical trainers of their children.[50]

43. Psalms 24:1 (NASB)
44. Deuteronomy 8:18 (NASB)
45. Proverbs 22:3 (NASB)
46. Matthew 25:14–28 (NASB)
47. 2 Corinthians 9:10–15 (NASB)
48. Matthew 6:24 (NASB)
49. Colossians 3:20 (NASB)
50. Proverbs 22:6 (NASB)

- As parents, husbands and wives are to be the counselors of their children.[51]

- As parents, husbands and wives must not provoke their children to wrath.[52]

The Problem:

As parents, husbands and wives must raise their children in the fear and admonishment of the Lord. Husbands and wives cannot exercise God-ordained authority to train, instruct, discipline, counsel, and encourage their children on how to glorify and love God and others apart from Christ.

> Fathers, do not provoke your children to anger, but bring them up in the discipline and instruction of the Lord.[53]

Point 11:

Husbands and wives must establish and maintain sexual unity:[54]

- Sexual unity honors and glorifies God.[55]

- It is the responsibility of the husband and the wife to satisfy each other sexually and not themselves only.[56]

- Sex is one way to express love to your spouse.

- True love involves giving.[57]

- The sexual union serves as an example of the unity of becoming one flesh.

51. 1 Thessalonians 5:14 (NASB)
52. Ephesians 6:4 (NASB)
53. Ephesians 6:4 (NASB)
54. Genesis 2:23–25 (NASB
55. Hebrews 13:4 (NASB)
56. 1 Corinthians 6:18–20, 7:3–5 (NASB)
57. John 3:16 (NASB)

The Problem:

Sexual unity in marriage begins with the giving of oneself to one's spouse.[58] A husband and wife can't become intimate with one another in a way that pleases God without first having an intimate relationship with God through Christ.[59]

> The husband must fulfill his duty to his wife, and likewise also the wife to her husband. The wife does not have authority over her own body, but the husband does; and likewise also the husband does not have authority over his own body, but the wife does.[60]

The Keys to a Successful Marriage is a Commitment, of the Husband and Wife, to Walk in Christ:

So what does it mean to be in Christ?:

First, let's discuss why the Gospel is significant as it relates to marriage. Having a marriage that reflects the image of God requires divine intervention. Therefore, the Gospel of Christ is significant because you and your spouse cannot have a marriage according to God's design apart from Christ! Why not? Because of sin!

What is sin?:

- It is living a godless, self-centered life based upon feelings!
- Sin is thinking, being, desiring, or doing what God forbids.
- It is the transgression of the law.[61]
- It is missing the mark of God's perfect standard.[62]
- It is dethroning God and exalting self!

The condition of the natural man from a biblical perspective:

58. 1 Corinthians 7:1–5 (NASB)
59. Colossians 3:12–14; 1 John 4 (NASB)
60. 1 Corinthians 7:3–4 (NASB)
61. 1 John 3:4; James 2:10; Romans 7:7, 8:7 (NASB)
62. Romans 14:23; 1 John 5:10; James 4:17; Isaiah 53:6 (NASB)

- His condition: the natural man is totally depraved.[63] He is instinctively in bondage to unrighteousness and wickedness and is incapable of rescuing himself.[64]

- His "heart" (thoughts, passions, affections, and desires) is naturally corrupt, desperately sick, deceitful, and wicked.[65]

The result of man's depraved condition:

- He is under God's wrath.[66]

- He is condemned by the law.[67]

- He is guilty of sin against God.

- The wages of sin is death.

Question:

Can you imagine what it would be like to spend your life living with a self-centered spouse, who has no desire to please God, always goes against what is right, and is puffed-up with pride? This person is a sinner. Keep in mind that you and your spouse are two sinners who have said, "I Do!"

What Does It Mean to Be in Christ?:

The Salvation of Being in Christ:

Jesus Christ is our Savior! The Gospel: I Corinthians 15:1–4. What are the ingredients of the Gospel?

> Now I make known to you, brethren, the Gospel which I preached to you, which also you received, in which also you stand, by which also you are saved, if you hold fast the word which I preached to you, unless you believed in vain. For I delivered to you as of first importance what I also received, that Christ died for our sins

63. Romans 1, 3 (NASB)

64. Romans 5, 6 (NASB)

65. Jeremiah 17:9; Matthew 12:34, 15:15–20; Mark 7:20–23 (NASB)

66. Romans 1:18 (NASB)

67. Galatians 3:13; 4:5; Romans 6:13, 16–19 (NASB)

according to the Scriptures, and that He was buried, and that He was raised on the third day according to the Scriptures[68]

Hope is a by-product of God grace obtainable through faith that stems from embracing the Gospel of Jesus Christ[69]

Is there hope for sinful man and woman to be saved?:

- He must be regenerated: Regeneration means "to impart life." It is the act by which God imparts life to the believer. It literally means to be born again.
- He must believe by faith that Jesus Christ is the son of God.[70]
- Through Christ, he is justified: justification means to declare righteous the one who has faith in Jesus Christ.
- Since we have been justified, our purpose now in life is to please God by being Christ-like.[71]
- The indwelling presence and power of the Holy Spirit enables him to understand and obey God's word.[72]
- Through Christ, he has received the gift of everlasting life.[73]

The Character of a Husband and Wife who are in Christ:

The Fruit of the Spirit:

But the fruit of the Spirit is love, joy, peace, patience, kindness, goodness, faithfulness, gentleness, self-control; against such things there is no law. Now those who belong to Christ Jesus have crucified the flesh with its passions and desires.[74]

68. 1 Corinthians 15:1–5 (NASB)
69. Ephesians 2:8–9 (NASB)
70. John 3:16; Romans 10:9 (NASB)
71. Romans 8:29; 1 Corinthians 6:11–12 (NASB)
72. 1 Corinthians 2:12–13 (NASB)
73. Romans 6:23 (NASB)
74. Galatians 5:22–24 (NASB)

Loving God and Others:

So, as those who have been chosen of God, holy and beloved, put on a heart of compassion, kindness, humility, gentleness and patience; bearing with one another, and forgiving each other, whoever has a complaint against anyone; just as the Lord forgave you, so also should you. Beyond all these things put on love, which is the perfect bond of unity.[75]

Walking in Wisdom that Produces Humility:

Who among you is wise and understanding? Let him show by his good behavior his deeds in the gentleness of wisdom.[76]

But the wisdom from above is first pure, then peaceable, gentle, reasonable, full of mercy and good fruits, unwavering, without hypocrisy. And the seed whose fruit is righteousness is sown in peace by those who make peace.[77]

The Blessings of a Husband and Wife who are in Christ:

Blessed be the God and Father of our Lord Jesus Christ, who has blessed us with every spiritual blessing in the heavenly places in Christ, just as He chose us in Him before the foundation of the world, that we would be holy and blameless before Him. In love He predestined us to adoption as sons through Jesus Christ to Himself, according to the kind intention of His will, to the praise of the glory of His grace, which He freely bestowed on us in the Beloved. In Him we have redemption through His blood, the forgiveness of our trespasses, according to the riches of His grace which He lavished on us. In all wisdom and insight He made known to us the mystery of His will, according to His kind intention which He purposed in Him with a view to an administration suitable to the fullness of the times, that is, the summing up of all things in Christ, things in the heavens and things on the earth. In Him also

75. Colossians 3:12–14 (NASB)
76. James 3:13 (NASB)
77. James 3:17–18 (NASB)

we have obtained an inheritance, having been predestined according to His purpose who works all things after the counsel of His will, to the end that we who were the first to hope in Christ would be to the praise of His glory. In Him, you also, after listening to the message of truth, the Gospel of your salvation—having also believed, you were sealed in Him with the Holy Spirit of promise[78]

According to Ephesians 1:3–13, in Christ you are:

- Blessed: to show favor. Christ intervened in our lives for our good and God's glory.
- Chosen: to be selected, to be preferred, called, to be picked, to be elected.
- Predestined: to be declared, decreed, and determined beforehand to do something.
- Adopted: to be received into a relationship as a child, a person who was once a stranger is now accepted and regarded as a member of God's family.
- Recipients of grace: God's unmerited favor; a favor done without expectation of reciprocation or return.
- Redeemed: to be set free from the captivity of sin, through the payment of a ransom.
- Forgiven: to be released for the penalty of sin; to be pardoned and reinstated in a relationship and fellowship.
- An inheritance: a birthright, a heritage, or to be entitled to a portion of an estate by choice of the owner of the estate.
- Hope: the hope of salvation through Christ.
- Sealed: to secure for safe delivery; salvation and an inheritance that is secure and safe and cannot be revoked or nullified.

Summary:

How does one move from chaos in marriage to conformity to Christ? The keys to a successful marriage is to walk in Christ and the pursuit of Christ-likeness because man and woman were created for that purpose. To walk

78. Ephesians 1:3–13 (NASB)

in Christ is to walk according to wisdom that comes from God. James says, "But the wisdom from above is first pure, then peaceable, gentle, reasonable, full of mercy and good fruits, unwavering, without hypocrisy. And the seed whose fruit is righteousness is sown in peace by those who make peace."[79] When a husband and wife exemplify these character qualities, it produces a joyful and peaceful marriage that is void of misery.

79. James 3:17–18 (NASB)

Appendix A

Survey on Identifying Differences and Personal Preferences

MY SPOUSE AND I are different. Husbands and wives are different. You and I are different. How are you and your spouse different? Complete the following survey and identify ways in which you and your spouse are different. Choose appropriate descriptions that best describe you and your spouse. Schedule a time to compare and discuss your answers, as well as the application questions, with your spouse.

Appendix A

How are you and your spouse different in the following areas?	Him:	Her:
Showing affection: Enjoys touching, hugs, or holding hands. Not touchy-feely; need my space.		
Decision-making: Just get it done—quick decision-maker. Likes to make decisions then move on without much thought. Slow to decide, considers all options; ponders "what if" even after a decision is made.		
Personality: Laid Back Driven Fast Slow Talkative Quiet Domineering Passive		
Resolving problems: Let's discuss it, deal with it, and fix it right now. Let's talk about it later because I need time to process it.		

Survey on Identifying Differences and Personal Preferences

How are you and your spouse different in the following areas?	Him:	Her:
Socializing: Extrovert; likes to talk to others; social butterfly; saddened when the party is over, and guests leave. Introvert; enjoys being alone. Happy when the party is over and glad to see folks leave.		
Spirituality: Spiritually mature; ready to serve in ministry. Spiritual disinterested; not really into church or the Bible. Similar Religious backgrounds. Different religious backgrounds.		
Sexual needs: Wants sex more often. Wants sex less often.		
Togetherness: Needs more romance, and enjoys spending quality time together. Not very romantic; wants more "me" time alone.		

Appendix A

How are you and your spouse different in the following areas?	Him:	Her:
Admission of wrongs: Quick to ask for forgiveness and take responsibility for wrongdoing. Refuse to admit faults, or rarely ask for forgiveness.		
Expression of feelings: Externalizes; direct and quick in expressing feelings. Internalizes; reluctant to share how one really feels.		
Response to conflict: Confrontational; easily expresses irritation and displeasure. Non-confrontational; shuts down and avoids confrontation to keep the peace.		
Finances: A spender; concerned about the here and now. A saver; concerned about the future.		
Historical backgrounds: Raised by both parents. Raised by one parent. Raised by someone other than biological parents.		

Survey on Identifying Differences and Personal Preferences

How are you and your spouse different in the following areas?	Him:	Her:
Family relations: Came from a family who is close, and loving. Came from a family who is distant, and dysfunctional.		
In-laws: A good relationship with in-laws. Do not relate well with in-laws and keep my distance.		
Being on time: Being on time is essential; hate to be late. Being on time is not that important; is typically late, no big deal.		
Parenting: Strict with children; believes in administering discipline of some form. Permissive with children; talking to the children is sufficient without discipline.		
Education: Has a graduate degree. Has obtained an undergrad degree. High school diploma only.		

How are you and your spouse different in the following areas?	Him:	Her:
Making plans: Sporadic, likes surprises; no need to make plans; go with the flow; adventurous. Likes to make plans, needs structure; does not like surprises; is not adventurous.		
Communication styles: Talks a lot; dominates the conversations; gives lots of details; or does not always say what they mean. Talks less; straight to the point; does not provide enough details; means what they say.		

Application Questions:

1. Based on your answers on this survey, in what are areas are you and your spouse different? _____

   _____

   _____

2. Which ones are the most problematic for you and why? _____

   _____

   _____

3. How do you respond to your differences? _____

   _____

   _____

4. If your response is not the best, what do you need to do to change? If you are not sure, ask your spouse. _____

_____

_____

5. Are you willing to accept your differences even if your spouse refuses to change; why or why not? _____

_____

_____

6. If your spouse is unwilling to change, will you commit to having responses that are pleasing to God? _____

_____

_____

Pray that you can continue to love your spouse despite your differences and pray that you exhibit tolerance, longsuffering, patience, and kindness and that your spouse learns to show these same loving (Christ-like) attitudes toward you. Pray Colossians 3:12–14:

> So, as [one] who has been chosen of God, holy and beloved, [Help me to] put on a heart of compassion, kindness, humility, gentleness and patience; bearing with [Your spouse's name], and forgiving [My Spouse's name], [when I have] a complaint against [him or her]; just as the Lord forgave [me], so also should [I]. Beyond all these things [Help me to] *put on* love, which is the perfect bond of unity.[1]

---

1. Colossians 3:12–14 (NASB)

Appendix B

Identifying Unmet Expectations

WHAT ARE SOME THINGS you expect from your husband or wife? What are some of the things that you need from your spouse? What are some of your desires? Put a circle around each unmet expectation. Insert your list of expectations, desires, and needs on the "Resolving Unmet Expectations" worksheet.

My expectations of my wife:	My expectations of my husband:

My expectations of my wife:	My expectations of my husband:

How to Resolve Unmet Expectations:

Schedule time to do the following:

- Complete columns 1 and 2 in the following chart on the following page. Then give your form to your spouse and allow your spouse a few days to review your answers and complete their response in columns 3 through 5.

- Schedule a time to discuss what each of you has listed as your expectations and how the fulfillment of the expectation would look like in practice.

- If your interest is still unclear, ask questions for clarification, such as, "what do you expect, want, need, or desire of me as it relates to this specific item?"

- Listen without interrupting.

- Alternatively, you and your spouse are to share whether you believe your interest or expectation is reasonable; why or why not?

- Each of you are to discuss your ability and willingness to meet his or her expectation or to satisfy their interest.

- If you have chosen to comply, describe, from your perspective, what it would look like in practice.

- If you have chosen to compromise, then you all need to discuss what it would look like if you met each other have way.

- Both of you need to determine how your choice is going to affect the marriage if you chose to reject the expectation. Decide whether or not your choice violates biblical principles. If so, confess, repent, and walk in obedience.

- As your spouse make attempts to satisfy your expectations, make sure you affirm appreciation and thank them for their efforts. Be his or her cheerleader.

- You must commit to showing grace and gentle correction when your spouse occasionally falls short.

If your spouse refuses to comply, pray for them and yourself.

My Expectations:	My Expectations:	Your Spouse's Response:	Your Spouse's Response:	Your Spouse's Response:	Our Response:
1	2	3	4	5	6
What are my interests, expectations, needs, wants, or desires?	How does it look in practice?	Am I being reasonable?	Are you willing to comply, compromise, or reject?	Does your decision violate God's word?	If you reject, how will it affect our relationship?

My Expectations:	My Expectations:	Your Spouse's Response:	Your Spouse's Response:	Your Spouse's Response:	Our Response:
1	2	3	4	5	6
What are my interests, expectations, needs, wants, or desires?	How does it look in practice?	Am I being reasonable?	Are you willing to comply, compromise, or reject?	Does your decision violate God's word?	If you reject, how will it affect our relationship?
Ex: "I want you to listen to me more when I am talking."	"Make eye contact, give a nod, be attentive, and avoid distractions."				

Bibliography

"10 Ways to Rekindle the Passion in Your Marriage." The Gottman Institute, accessed March 8, 2021, https://www.gottman.com/blog/10-ways-rekindle-passion-marriage/.

Bridges, Charles. *A Commentary on Proverbs: Geneva Series of Commentaries*. Banner of Truth Trust, 2007.

Card, Orson Scott. *BrainyQuote.com*, accessed March 8, 2021, https://www.brainyquote.com/quotes/orson_scott_card_377074.

Collins English Dictionary, s.v. "intimacy," accessed March 7, 2021, https://www.collinsdictionary.com/us/dictionary/english/intimacy.

hrf. "55 Surprising Divorce Statistics for Second Marriages." https://healthresearchfunding.org/55-surprising-divorce-statistics-second-marriages/

Merriam-Webster.com Dictionary, s.v. "conflict," accessed March 7, 2021, https://www.merriam-webster.com/dictionary/conflict.

———. s.v. "quarrel," accessed March 7, 2021, https://www.merriam-webster.com/dictionary/quarrel.

PreachingToday. "Statistic: Jesus' Teachings on Money." https://www.preachingtoday.com/illustrations/1996/december/410.html.

Priolo, Lou. *The Heart of Anger: Practical Help for the Prevention and Cure of Anger in Children*. Amityville: Calvary, 1997.

Reuters Life! "German man chainsaws house in two after divorce split." https://www.reuters.com/article/us-germany-divorce-chainsaw/german-man-chainsaws-house-in-two-in-divorce-split-idUSL0920001720070309.

Solzhenitsyn, Alexander. *One Day in the Life of Ivan Denisovich*, New York: Signet, 2008.

Tan, Paul Lee. *Encyclopedia of 7700 Illustrations: A Treasury of Illustrations, Anecdotes, Facts, and Quotations for Pastors, Teachers, and Christian Workers*. Garland: Bible Communications, 1996.

Vine, William E. *Vine's Expository Dictionary of Old Testament and New Testament Words*. Nashville: Thomas Nelson, 1940.

Wevorce Team. "6 Surprising Statistics About Divorce in 2017." https://www.wevorce.com/blog/6-surprising-divorce-statistics-divorce-2017/.

"What We Want, What We Believe." National Women's Liberation, accessed March 8, 2021, https://womensliberation.org/want-believe/.

Zodhiates, Spiros. *The Complete Word Study Dictionary: New Testament*. Chattanooga: AMG, 2000.

www.ingramcontent.com/pod-product-compliance
Lightning Source LLC
Chambersburg PA
CBHW060330100426
42812CB00003B/941